Introduction

Places: Belfast

Places: Excursions

Culture

Practical Information

◁ **Grand Opera House (p28)** This oriental fantasy hosts all manner of theatrical events: West End musicals, Shakespeare, Van Morrison concerts — and even the odd opera.

▷ **Titanic heritage (p54)** The doomed liner that sank in 1912 was built here and is the focus of tours and a festival celebrating shipbuilding.

◁ **Botanic Gardens (p52)** Colourful park with a classic Palm House and Tropical Ravine.

▷ **Parliament Buildings (p76)** Designed to echo Buckingham Palace, Stormont is the setting for Northern Ireland's elusive devolved government.

◁ **Giant's Causeway (p86)** One of the wonders of the world, this is an astonishing array of more than 40,000 basalt columns, mostly hexagonals, formed by the cooling of molten lava. Nearby are many fine uncrowded beaches.

△ **Ulster Folk and Transport Museum (p78)** Cottages and cars, traditions and trains. A fascinating collection.

△ **City Hall (p33)** This shameless imitation of St Paul's Cathedral dominates the city centre.

▷ **Crown Liquor Saloon (p29)** This Victorian bar is so ornate that the National Trust bought it.

◁ **Derry's Walls (p89)** Europe's last walled city, famously beseiged in 1689 and now centre of an exhilarating social and cultural scene.

▷ **Antrim Coast Road (p84)** Spectacular drive by the sea, taking in alluring fishing villages such as Cushendun.

Belfast – Titanic Town

Without its baggage of troubles, and the resultant 30 years of media coverage which sent its flames around the globe, Belfast could have been seen in another light: as an extravagance of pubs and churches; as a seaport rich in Victorian buildings on the western edge of Europe where they built the ill-fated *Titanic*; as the home of Irish linen; as host to Nobel Laureate poet Seamus Heaney's campus, George Best's schooldays, Van Morrison's streets, and a liquor saloon preserved as a national monument and immortalised in *Odd Man Out*, Carol Reed's 1947 film noir starring James Mason as a wounded Irish rebel on the run.

But such attractions were not promoted in the 1950s and '60s. The Unionist governments of the time dissociated themselves from all that was marketable to visitors as being in any way Irish. Their tourist literature listed which minor British royal opened which public building but gave scant mention of the abundant *craic*, of the in-your-face northern humour, of pubs pulsing with music, of Guinness downed in the Crown Liquor Saloon with the cockles and mussels that have been gathered with relish from the surrounding sea loughs since Mesolithic peoples settled here 8,000 years ago.

From the 1970s to the 1990s the word 'Belfast' was associated with car bombs and rioting. Today, the climate has changed dramatically: you can stroll fearlessly past fashionable chain stores and hip hotels, you can dance the night away at cutting-edge clubs, you can eat and drink remarkably well, and set off on excursions to explore some of the finest scenery in the British Isles.

Opposite: Belfast in 1911, with Titanic in the background
Below: singer Van Morrison – a blue plaque adorns his childhood home in East Belfast

LOCATION AND GEOGRAPHY

Belfast sits in a saucer of hills in the north-east of Ireland, at the head of a broad sea lough at the mouth of the River Lagan, which flows east into the Irish Sea. It is the capital of the six counties of Northern Ireland (Antrim, Armagh, Derry, Down, Fermanagh and Tyrone), since 1921 an integral part of the United Kingdom of Great Britain and Northern Ireland. On a

Below: festival fireworks over the River Lagan
Bottom: Hallowe'en parade

clear day, from the lough's mouth, you can see Scotland 30km (20 miles) to the east. Dublin, capital of the 26-county Republic of Ireland, lies 160km (100 miles) to the south.

Although Northern Ireland occupies just 17 percent of the island's landmass, it contains a high proportion of its physical attractions. The Antrim Coast Road is an engineering marvel. Behind it lie the nine Glens of Antrim, a world of rugged scenery and weather-beaten farmers. On the northern coast, past long stretches of sandy beaches lies the Giant's Causeway, a remarkable geological curiosity. The lakeland of County Fermanagh is a playground for boat enthusists and fishermen. Water sports are popular on Lough Neagh, the largest sheet of inland water in the British Isles. In Country Down, the often serenaded Mourne Mountains attract walkers. And then there are the 80 golf courses…

CLIMATE

At 67m (217ft) above sea level, Belfast lies 54°39N, 6°13W – as far north as Canada's Labrador and Denmark's Copenhagen, and as far west as Land's End and the Isle of Skye. The Gulf Stream delivers a daytime average of 18°C (65°F) in the sunniest months of June, July and August, with six hours of sunshine. Occasionally in July, temperatures reach 30°C (low 80s°F), but on summer nights the thermometer drops to 11°C (50°F) and winter minimum temperatures average 2°C (36°F).

April and May are the driest months, with 2in (50mm) each of the year's rainfall of 33in (84cm). But you can meet all the seasons in one day, so it's always prudent to pack a raincoat and sweater.

POPULATION

More than a fifth of Northern Ireland's 1½ million population lives in Belfast itself, with another 175,000 in the Belfast area. Roughly two-thirds are Protestants, descendants of the settlers planted in the region by England's James I in the early 17th century. Like monarchs before and after him, James saw Ireland as a back door through which Spain or France could invade England and was prepared to use military might to ensure this did not happen.

Apart from a small Chinese population of 4,000 or so, mostly in the restaurant trade, Belfast had little experience of immigration. Recently blacks and eastern Europeans have settled in the city, provoking a number of racist attacks.

THE ULSTER CHARACTER

Instead of the soft, beguiling brogue that the world regards as distinctively Irish, the Northern Irish accent is harder, less melodious. Think Van Morrison rather than Enya. Some say it is an accent that adapts particularly well to rabble-rousing oratory, as ear-splittingly exemplified by the province's most successful politician, the Reverend Ian Paisley.

Nor does the people's character conform with the Hollywood image of Irishness. Northern Protestants are generally regarded as being more earnest and less imaginative than Northern Catholics, who are in turn judged to be less outgoing and less impulsive than their Southern counterparts.

Stubbornness and a reluctance to compromise are more often seen as virtues rather than vices, and there were times during the 1970s and '80s that even fervent nationalists in the Republic questioned the wisdom of encouraging these feuding tribes to become fellow citizens in a united Ireland. Nevertheless, visitors are constantly surprised to encounter a warm and gregarious welcome in Northern Ireland – as long, of course, as the talk doesn't turn to politics.

BEGINNINGS

Wave after wave of cultures sailed up Belfast Lough, raiding, trading, intermarrying. The Celts

Divided loyalties
A Northern Irish citizen is entitled to choose either a British passport or an Irish passport. This disputed question of identity has underpinned much violence over the years. Yet, even where community relations are good, the two main tribes tend to live in separate areas. This separation was partly dictated the needs of education. The Roman Catholic church traditionally insisted that Catholic children attended Catholic schools, where they played Gaelic games and were taught the Irish language and culture. Protestants attended Protestant schools, played rugby and cricket and followed a largely British curriculum. Because most people settled near their own church and school, the two sides remained strangers.

The Siege of Enniskillen in 1594 was a typical assault by English forces on the castle of a local chieftain

👁 **English Overtures**
In 1177 John de Courcy, a minor landowner from the north of England, sailed into Belfast with his mailed and mounted Anglo-Norman army. He annexed Ulster against the wish of his monarch, Henry II, who knew that John would become its sovereign in all but title. But de Courcy never subdued the chieftains and was later ejected from Ulster by King John. Celt and Norman intermarried, forming a new land-owning Catholic class, the Old English.

New technology created a thriving textiles industry in the 18th century.

landed 7,000 years after the Neolithic hunter-gatherers, ushering in the Iron Age. No-one is sure about the Romans' involvement, if any, but St Patrick's landfall was in AD432, 50km (30 miles) southeast. Two centuries later comes the first mention of Belfast when the Celts noted their predecessors, the Cruithin and Uliad, battling at Béal Feirste, 'the approach to the sandbank ford', on the River Lagan. By 900, Vikings were dragging their boats over the sandbank.

ENGLISH ADVENTURERS

A Scot, Edward the Bruce, came up the lough in 1315, to be crowned king and die in battle. From then on, Belfast's English garrisoned castle was destroyed, rebuilt, demolished, retaken. England's Elizabeth I, knowing Ireland would side with Catholic Spain, needed to lay waste the Catholic chieftains. Her first attack on Belfast was easily repulsed in 1571 by O'Neills holding this wooded, impenetrable, Gaelic-speaking valley in their fiefdom. But in 1573 her favourite, the Earl of Essex, beat them, quartering survivors during his victory banquet, but failing to build a lasting town. The place fell, in 1603, to an even more ruthless criminal adventurer, Sir Arthur Chichester.

It was Chichester who created Belfast, populating it in 1606 with Scots Dissenter tradesmen, some of whose descendants 30 years later set sail for the Americas conscious that, although the Catholic Irish were at the bottom of the privi-

lege ladder, they themselves were no more than second-class citizens. Protestants (established church), Dissenters (Presbyterian) and Catholics were the divisions that persisted through another 200 years of skirmish, and set the demographic patterns for recent troubles.

Chichester's followers sided with the Crown in the English Civil War but Belfast fell in 1648 to a superior Scots army on Parliament's side. The town's leaders made another mistake, welcoming the accession of James II , a Catholic – but they changed their mind when he insisted on pro-Catholic policies. James seized the town in 1689, but it was soon regained by William of Orange. William, a Dutch Protestant, had married James's daughter Mary; English nobles invited the couple to replace James on the English throne.

A US consulate was established in Belfast in 1796 and, fired by the spirit of the American and French Revolutions, Belfast's Dissenter middle class led the doomed 1798 rebellion, designed to free the entire island from British rule. But French troops, on whom they counted, never made it north. In 1800 the Act of Union in 1800 dissolved Ireland's Parliament and created the United Kingdom of Great Britain and Ireland.

THE ROOTS OF SECTARIANISM

Sectarianism took hold. When Catholics began buying up land in Ulster, Protestants formed a vigilante outfit, the Peep o' Day Boys, to burn out Catholics in dawn raids. The Catholics retaliated with their own vigilante force, the Defenders.

In 1795 a bitter clash between the two groups at the Battle of the Diamond, near Armagh, left 30 dead. The Protestants, fearing worse was to come, reorganised as the Orange Society, named after William of Orange. Thus entrenched, Catholics and Protestants battled for centuries for their slice of an inadequate economic cake.

THE INDUSTRIAL HERITAGE

French (Protestant) Huguenots fleeing persecution brought linen to the banks of the River Lagan, but it was still a cottage industry when Presbyterians, ushering in the Industrial Revolution, imported power-driven cotton machinery in 1771. Soon the

Below: Walter Devereux, 1st Earl of Essex, was despatched in the 1570s by Elizabeth I to colonise northeastern Ireland

Bottom: William of Orange, who defeated James I at the Battle of the Boyne in 1690, remains to this day a potent icon of Ulster Unionism

population was 27,832, the majority employed in mills. Protestant spinners were well paid, Catholic weavers not. Trade was volatile, firms ruthless, unions illegal, unemployment high, housing intolerable, typhus and cholera inevitable, strikes and protests frequent.

Facing quality competition, Irish cotton was in trouble by the 1830s. But economic revival came with the industrialisation of linen, the railway age, and port improvements. By 1856 Mulholland's linen works was the world's largest. When the 1864 American Civil War cut off cotton supplies, linen flourished, bringing prosperity for owners and a 15-hour day for workers.

In 1853 Edward Harland, who trained under George Stephenson of *Rocket* fame, hired Belfast's skilled labour, at low wages, to build iron, not wooden, ships. By the 1870s Harland & Wolff was the world's largest shipbuilder, linked to the White Star Line, which shipped emigrants to America. Their *Oceanic* broke transatlantic records, but the *Titanic* sank on its maiden voyage in 1912. A spin-off, Belfast Ropeworks, became a world leader. Gallaher's Tobacco, Irish Distillers, plus tea and ventilation plants followed. Belfast had become Ireland's only industrial city.

THE CHICHESTERS

The industrial revolution was facilitated by a change in land ownership. Until the mid-19th century, Belfast was the only Irish town to be run as a private fiefdom by a single family, lying as it did within the Donegall estate in Co. Antrim, owned by Sir Arthur Chichester's descendants.

The first marquis of Donegall, though he lived in England, was enlightened enough to fund fine public buildings and insist on decent architectural standards. His spendthrift son, who succeeded to the estates in 1799, continued this policy but ran up such huge debts that he was forced to start selling off leases. By 1855 virtually the whole town had been sold to tenants or rich speculators.

The family's legacy is the streets in Belfast named after them. A descendant, Arthur Chichester-Clark, a country gentleman, was Northern Ireland's prime minister in 1969 when British troops were called in to stop sectarian violence.

Below: Orangemen opposed to Britain's granting Home Rule to Ireland march on Belfast City Hall in 1886
Bottom: Sir Edward Carson, the brilliant lawyer who had helped convict Oscar Wilde, led the Ulster Protestants' campaign to remain British

NORTHERN IRELAND IS BORN

World War I (1914–18) saved Ireland from imminent civil war. Thousands of armed militants on both sides joined up and the city prospered in the war effort. Dublin's Easter Rising of 1916 failed, but the Anglo-Irish War of 1919–21 led to a treaty setting up the Irish Free State. However, Protestant resistance in the northeast promised such bloodshed that the politicans compromised, carving out six of the nine counties of the province of Ulster which would be called Northern Ireland and would remain part of Britain.

Although the northeastern counties had been the only part of Ireland to become industralised, the long decline of traditional industries such as shipbuilding and textiles had begun and there were never enough jobs or decent houses to go round. Unionist politicians ensured that their supporters got the pick of what was available. Many northern nationalists, by refusing on principle to participate in the 'illegitimate' state's public affairs, offered little resistance. The British government, glad to be rid of the troublesome Irish Question, ignored the discrimination and gerrymandering endemic in their forgotten province.

THE TROUBLES

So it might have continued, with occasional bouts of sectarian violence, had not the 1947 Education Act delivered university education on merit, not privilege. Students swelled the ranks of the

A Difficult Birth

Nationalists vowed in 1921 to strangle the six-county Northern Ireland at birth. But their attention was diverted by civil war in the 26 counties of the new Free State, where opinion was bitterly divided over the terms of the treaty that divided the island. Unionists in the North lost no time in making Belfast, Northern Ireland's capital, the seat of 'a Protestant parliament for a Protestant people' (as its first prime minister, James Craig, put it).

Below: a nationalist mural
Bottom: Belfast circa 1910

👁 **Belfast's Bosses**
Although the political opponents elected to the Northern Ireland Assembly found it hard to sit at the same table, the same is not true of those elected to Belfast City Council. Once dominated by Unionists, the council's membership now reflects the city's divisions, yet business gets done. The Democratic Unionist Party holds 15 of the 51 seats, closely followed by Sinn Féin with 14. Other Unionist and nationalist parties are more or less matched.

Civil Rights Movement which, inspired by the spirit of 1968 which swept American and French campuses, marched to demand a fair allocation of public housing and jobs to Catholics.

Hard-line Unionists such as the Rev. Ian Paisley – a firebrand preacher and founder in 1951 of the fundamentalist Free Presbyterian Church – had warned of Catholic subversion throughout the 1960s and saw the protests as an insurrection. The Unionist government agreed and turned water cannons and police truncheons on the marchers in full view of the world's media. Civil unrest began to engulf Northern Ireland. As old animosities flared up, Protestants began setting fire to Catholics' houses in Belfast. A moribund IRA resurrected itself to defend them. Protestant terrorist groups were formed in retaliation.

PEACE BREAKS OUT

It took 30 years, the abolition of the local parliament, the imposition of direct rule from Westminster, the creation of a Dublin–London political axis, major population shifts and the loss of more than 3,200 lives before the province voted in 1998 for peace through a power-sharing Assembly.

The fact that Martin McGuinness, a former IRA leader in Derry, became Minister of Education – in charge of the teaching of both Protestant and Catholic children – seemed to symbolise the remarkable progress that had been made. But mutual suspicions remained and political deadlock forced the British government to suspend the Assembly until trust could be established.

The Rev Ian Paisley preaching the word in the late 1960s

A NEW BELFAST

Neither planners nor bombers were kind to Belfast. In the 1960s a lacklustre provincial civil service failed to recognise the unique vernacular environment that the architect Charles Lanyon *(see page 107)* had created a century before. Great buildings were demolished, replaced by flaking concrete. The bombers had a go at much that was left, leaving a city rich in unplanned parking lots with a few score of fine buildings standing out.

With the first inklings of peace, hide-bound planners swept flyovers through inner-city villages, and Belfast rekindled its affection for its

potent Victorian and scant Georgian heritage.
Laganside Corporation rediscovered Lagan's
banks and captured a public imagination fired
by Victor Robinson's keynote Waterfront Hall and
plans for a cobbled Cathedral cultural quarter.
Vast amounts of plate glass suggested that the
architectural profession at least was persuaded
that the car bomb was a thing of the past.

From the City Hall south to the University,
streets became packed with café-bars and disco-
pubs. Clubbers from Britain and further afield discovered that Belfast had a vibrant nightlife, and
the growth of low-cost airlines enabled them to
sample it. The city even hosted the British Council of Shopping Centres' annual conference.

POWER SHARING RETURNS

But would consumerism prove more enticing than
sectarianism? The decisive moment came after an
election in 2007 which was dominated by Unionist support for the Democratic Unionist Party, led
by the Rev. Ian Paisley, and equally decisive
nationalist support for Sinn Féin, led by Gerry
Adams. Could the two bitterly opposed parties
finally agree to run Northern Ireland together in
a durable power-sharing assembly?

It was touch-and-go, but five years of direct rule
from London came to an end on 8 May when Ian
Paisley and Sinn Féin's Martin McGuinness, who
had never talked to each other before, sat down
together as Northern Ireland's new leaders.

Below: Belfast Festival gives a leg-up to the city's lighter side
Bottom: Sinn Féin leader Gerry Adams backs the 1998 Good Friday Agreement

HISTORICAL HIGHLIGHTS

7,000BC The Ice Age retreats. Mesolithic peoples gather cockles from River Lagan mudbanks.

3,000BC Neolithic peoples build Giant's Ring dolmen near Belfast.

500BC Celts name this place Béal Feirste, Belfast, 'approach to the sandbank ford'.

AD432 St Patrick lands at Saul.

666 Belfast's first mention in history books: a battle at the ford between Cruithin and Uliad.

1014 Brian Ború, High King of Ireland, defeats the Vikings after a century of marauding.

1177 Celtic foot soldiers stand little chance against the horsemen of Anglo-Norman adventurer John de Courcy, who fords the river at Belfast against Henry II's express instruction.

1315 Scot Edward the Bruce invades with 6,000 men to be crowned king and die in battle.

1523 The Fitzgeralds 'brake a castell called Belfast' in 1523 as they did in 1512 and 1503, as did O'Donnells in 1489 and O'Neills in 1476.

1571 O'Neill repulses Queen Elizabeth I's attack on Belfast, the first attempt at the bloody colonisation of Catholic Ulster, the most Gaelic and impenetrable of Ireland's four provinces and a possible ally to Spain's maritime ambition.

1573 The Earl of Essex is gifted Belfast.

1597 Shane O'Neill takes the English in Belfast Castle, slitting throats and disembowelling.

1603 Sir Arthur Chichester is granted 'castle of Bealfaste' and founds a prosperous settlement.

1606 Protestant Lowland Scots settlers are imported, bringing their trades and industry.

1607 Ireland's princes flee the north, to Spain.

1613 Belfast's charter of incorporation places it in the fortunes of the Chichesters for 200 years.

1648 Belfast, loyal to the Crown, falls to Scots siding with Parliament in the English Civil War.

1649 Cromwell takes Belfast by siege. The city is retaken by the Royalists in 1660.

1685 The Protestant Corporation's welcome to Catholic James II is short-lived. James takes the undefended city in 1689, but William III's forces regain it in August that year.

1690 William of Orange arrives, then marches south to defeat James at the Battle of the Boyne.

1756 The first food riots occur.

1757 5th Earl of Donegall leases off Belfast. Protests as developers charge exorbitant rents.

1760 The French capture Carrickfergus.

1773 John Wesley describes the plight of Belfast's destitutes. Poorhouse planned.

1776 St Anne's Church is completed.

1777 Assembly Rooms complete. Henry Joy McCracken brings in cotton industry, and introduces the industrial revolution to Belfast.

1778 *John Paul Jones*, an American privateer, engages *HMS Drake* in Belfast Lough, inspiring Presbyterians to form 1st Volunteer Company seeking independence for Irish parliament.

1791 Society of the United Irishmen is launched.

1795 The Orange Order is founded.

1796 US consulate established in Belfast.

1798 Rebellion of Presbyterian-led United Irishmen is crushed. Henry Joy McCracken is hanged. Wexford revolt. Wolfe Tone commits suicide.

1800 Act of Union dissolves the Irish Parliament and creates the United Kingdom of Great Britain and Ireland.

1828 The decision is made to build Belfast's first power-driven linen mill.

1832 Cholera epidemic. Hercules Street riots between Orangemen and Catholics mark the beginning of centuries of disturbances on 12 July.

1839 Ulster Railway Company launched.

1845 Charles Lanyon refurbishes Belfast Exchange, launching his architectural career.

1846 Famine victims flock to Belfast. Typhus ensues. Soup kitchens open.

1849 Queen Victoria pays a visit, but the city corporation mis-spells the Irish for 'Hundred Thousand Welcomes'. Cholera strikes.

1857 July's sectarian riots put down by Hussars.

1863 Gallagher's Tobacco factory opened.

1887 First pneumatic tyre invented in Belfast.

1888 Belfast receives royal charter as a city.

1892 Home Rule (for Ireland) Bill defeated.

1912 The *Titanic*, Belfast built and designed, sinks. On 28 September, 471,414 predominantly Protestant Ulsterfolk sign Solemn League and Covenant opposing impending Home Rule.

1913 100,000 Covenantors join Ulster Volunteer Force under rebel British general. A (Unionist) provisional government is devised. British navy to blockade Belfast. Irish-based British officers mutiny. Arms for the UVF arrive by the ton.

1914 World War I diverts attention from Home Rule and saves Ulster from a civil war.

1916 Dublin's Easter Rising, inspired by Belfast wing of Irish Republican Brotherhood, is suppressed. In the war, the Ulster Division loses 5,000 men on the Somme battlefield on 1 July.

1920 Recession fires riots, curbed by curfew.

1921 Six counties of Northern Ireland remain in the UK as rest of the island becomes 26-county Irish Free State, renaming itself as Éire in 1937, declaring its neutrality in World War II, and becoming the Republic of Ireland in 1949.

1932 Unemployment following Wall Street crash, provokes city riots.

1941 German bombing of Belfast. 700 dead.

1956 Ineffectual six-year IRA campaign begins.

1968–9 Civil rights marches suppressed. Civil unrest worsens. British troops intervene.

1971 The Chichesters finally bow out as James Chichester Clark, the Prime Minister, resigns.

1972 13 demonstrators are shot dead by British paratroopers on 'Bloody Sunday' in Derry City. Parliament in Belfast is abolished and direct rule from Westminster is imposed. More than 3,200 will die violently in the next 25 years.

1993 Secret peace talks begin with Britain.

1998 71 percent of voters back self-governing all-party Assembly, but terrorists refuse to hand in weapons, slowing the peace process.

1999 A power-sharing Assembly meets at Stormont, but is suspended in 2000, reinstated in 2002, then suspended again.

2004 A £26 million bank robbery is blamed on the IRA and keeps the Assembly suspended.

2005 The IRA says its war is over, its weapons destroyed. Protestant leaders are sceptical.

2007 After an election dominated by the Democratic Unionists and Sinn Féin, the two parties form a devolved, power-sharing government.

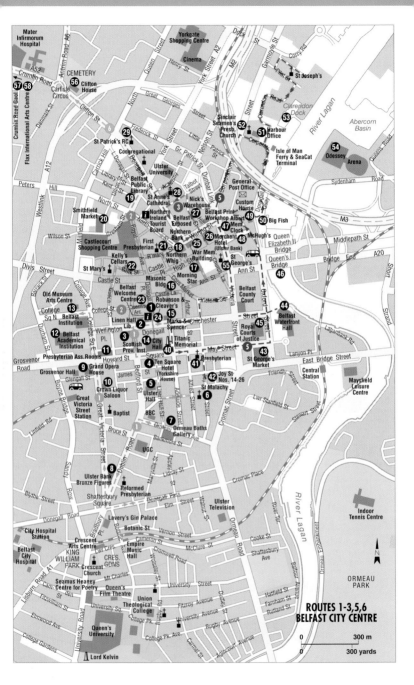

ROUTES 1-3,5,6
BELFAST CITY CENTRE

0 _____ 300 m
0 _____ 300 yards

1: The City Centre

Linen Hall Library – Donegall Square – Ulster Hall – Dublin Road – Donegall Pass – Shaftesbury Square – Grand Opera House – Crown Liquor Saloon – Old Museum – Wellington Place

It makes sense to visit the **Belfast and Northern Ireland Welcome Centre ❶** (47 Donegall Place, tel: 9024 6609) before starting this route. You can book tickets for concerts, theatre and accommodation and check out the entertainment scene. If you've got luggage, leave it here while you walk around the city.

LINEN HALL LIBRARY

Just around the corner, opposite the City Hall, at 17 Donegall Square North, the **★★Linen Hall Library ❷** (tel: 9032 1707, Mon–Fri 9.30am–5.30pm, Sat 9.30am–1pm) is the last public subscription library left in Ireland. Once occupying the White Linen Hall, on the site of the present City Hall, it has played a vigorous part in Belfast's cultural life for two centuries now. Thomas Russell, a founder member and the first librarian, was arrested at its earlier premises in Ann Street for his part in the United Irishmen uprising of 1798.

Within a hundred years the library had moved across to its present location, a three-storey, five-bay building with stucco mouldings on its windows. The most eminent of the architects who created Victorian Belfast, Charles Lanyon, designed the building as a linen warehouse of greyish-yellowish brick with a dressing of

Star Attraction
● **Linen Hall Library**

Telephone numbers
Telephone numbers in this book should be preceded by the code 028 if dialled from Britain and 44-28 if dialled from overseas.

Preceding pages: the view over City Hall
Below: Belfast Welcome Centre
Bottom: Linen Hall Library

Map on page 20

Researching Narnia
Linen Hall Library has added a collection of books by or about C. S. Lewis (1898–1963), the Belfast-born-and-raised Christian writer and author of the Narnian Chronicles. Visitors can access all the collections, although only members can borrow books.

The Apartment Bar, symbol of the new, chic Belfast

Victorian detail upon its Georgian proportions. Inside, an impressive brass-railed stone staircase leads to the muted calm of arcane reading rooms redolent with the aromas of the book stacks, with walls lined with heavy wooden glass-fronted bookcases and stained-glass windows commemorating famous writers.

Sensitively restored in recent years, at no little cost, it now has a modern café, which also serves wine and beer, and a well-stocked shop of literary souvenirs.

The library is still a venue for regular cultural activities, including literary lectures, drama, poetry recitations and exhibitions, but its main attraction remains its unique collections. Chief amongst these is a major Irish and Local Studies collection but many visitors come for its unrivalled Northern Ireland political collection from the Troubles, now running to some quarter of a million items. Collated from all parties to the conflict, it also contains a comprehensive press cuttings service, periodicals and even stickers and badges.

CHERUBS AND CHIEFS

Just opposite, facing the west side of City Hall, you can trace the industrial heritage of Belfast from carvings high up on the pale Giffock sandstone of the vast **★★Scottish Provident Institution ❸** on Donegall Square West. The building has almost as much Edwardian pomp and presence as the City Hall. Cherubs work at their ABCs on a Gutenberg printing press, and easily identified are an anchor and hammer for shipbuilding, plus skeins of linen yarn and spinning wheel, the tools of ropemaking.

Below, less finely carved heads, copied from Thomas Fitzpatrick's work on what is now the Malmaison Hotel in Victoria Street, represent the peoples to which a commercially buoyant city exported its goods: an Englishman, benign and plump; an Asian tribal chief with his nose-ring; an African; an indigenous north American with high cheekbones.

In stark contrast to its venerable host, the **Apartment,** 2 Donegall Square West, within whose environs it has prospered for some years now, has become a rather overused symbol of the new, chic Belfast that has emerged from the Troubles. A stylish bar with an all-day menu, music at nights, and clear views of City Hall, its arrival in a city centre that had been almost redundant in terms of entertainment during the Troubles, signalled a new kind of venue for a younger generation more interested in cappuccino and cocktails than political arguments or sectarian division. Such has been the avalanche of cool clubs, bars and cafés ever since, it now seems almost reassuringly traditional.

THE £26 MILLION HEIST

At the corner of Donegall Square West and Wellington Street, a most unlikely new tourist attraction has emerged on the Black Taxi tour route. The headquarters of the **Northern Bank** was the victim of a £26 million bank heist, the biggest all-cash robbery in British history, in December 2004, an event which had serious implications for the peace process after it was alleged that the supposedly dormant IRA had been involved.

Yorkshire House, on the corner of Donegall Square South and Linenhall Street, was built in 1862 as a three-storey, 18-bay linen warehouse and features a series of Heroes' Heads between first-floor windows, including George Washington, Isaac Newton, Homer and Michelangelo. Now the building has been transformed into the luxurious new **Ten Square Hotel** ❹ *(see page 126)* with a popular bar and restaurant.

At 7 Linenhall Street is the latest venture of pioneering Belfast restaurateur Paul Rankin, **Roscoff Brasserie** *(see page 113)*. **Linen Hall House** at 13–19 Linenhall Street, built in 1855, spent much of its life serving the linen trade, as did No 40, and to the right in Franklin Street, Nos 25–27.

Turning left, it is easy to spot the sometimes polychrome one-time linen warehouses on Bedford Street, particularly the warm brown sandstone mass of **Ewart**

Star Attraction
● **Scottish Provident Institution**

Scottish Provident Institution, and a native American, one of its many carved heads

Map
on page
20

Star performers

The Ulster Hall hosts all kinds of concerts, from regular Ulster Orchestra visits to rock and pop stars, kickboxing tournaments, beer festivals and much else. Cult rockers will know that the Rolling Stones played the Hall in 1964 and that Led Zeppelin's Stairway to Heaven had its stage debut here in 1971. The Hall's massive Mulholland organ attracts a different fan base.

The fan-vaulted ceiling of St Malachy's Church

House (No 17), built as the Italian Renaissance palace for a linen dynasty.

ULSTER HALL

W.J. Barre, architect Charles Lanyon's great rival, designed the Italianate stucco of the ★★**Ulster Hall** ❺ (tel: 9032 3900). Completed in 1862 as a grand ballroom, it became the largest music hall in the British Isles, its airy spaciousness and excellent acoustics also providing a resounding platform for the rallies of the Irish nationalist politicians Charles Stewart Parnell and Patrick Pearse and one holding the opposite view, David Lloyd George, Britain's prime minister from 1916 to 1922.

The Ulster Hall closed in April 2007 for a major refurbishment which will bring its facilities up-to-date, while also restoring many original features. These include the return of paintings of Belfast, commissioned by the venue from local artist Joyce Carey in 1902. From late 2008, when it's expected to re-open, it will be the new home of the Ulster Orchestra.

Along from the Ulster Hall, the New York-style **Deane's Deli** and Parisian flavoured **Café Vin** are under the auspices of Belfast's only Michelin-starred chef, Michael Deane.

ST MALACHY'S CHURCH

Turning left into Clarence Street, we find the dusky red-brick exterior of the Roman Catholic ★**St Malachy's Church** ❻ (tel: 9032 1713) framed in the east. Designed by Thomas Jackson in 1880, this church,

romantic as a Sir Walter Scott novel, is a splendid, octagonally turreted castellated excursion into Tudor Gothic, its panelled door studded and topped with armorial shields. However, it is the church's interior that makes the stranger gasp.

The dazzling **fan-vaulted ceiling**, a confection of creamy and frothy plasterwork, has been likened to a wedding cake turned inside out. In fact, it is an echo of Henry VII's Chapel in Westminster Abbey. Many of the original unpolished Irish oak fittings have disappeared but the organ is a century and a half old.

The church's chief benefactor, Captain Thomas Griffiths, understood that it would become the city's Roman Catholic cathedral, which accounts for the extravagance of decoration. A memorial to Griffiths is just inside the porch. The oak spire has long since been demolished, the original bell from the front left turret cracked and melted down. A new bell installed in 1868 no longer tolls, for its resonance was claimed to interfere with the maturing of spirit in Dunville's Whiskey Distillery, which stood nearby.

Return west up Clarence Street, catch a glimpse of the Black Mountain in the distance, and take the second left south along Linenhall Street to emerge on to Ormeau Avenue where the city's reservoir once shimmered. Much of the south side of the Avenue was destroyed during the Troubles, the warehouse sites now turned into car parks.

ORMEAU BATHS GALLERY

The BBC's Broadcasting House is on the right, the low Queen Anne red-brick elegance of the **★★Ormeau Baths Gallery ❼** (tel: 9032 1402, Tues–Sat 10am–5.30pm) opposite. Originally the Ormeau Avenue Public Baths, its eastern half became one of the city's premier visual arts venues in 1995, where its four bright, white, airy arts spaces over two floors play host to contemporary Irish and touring art. Some of the world's most famous and influential artists have featured at the gallery, including Gilbert and George, Yoko Ono, Willie Doherty, Henri Cartier-Bresson, Helen Chadwick and Phil Collins. It has also provided an opportunity for talented Irish artists to showcase their work, with Victor Sloan, Alistair MacLennan, Barbara Freeman, Willie McKeown, and Cecily Brennan just a handful who have made their mark here. On most Saturdays there are workshops for children and families.

Star Attractions
● **Ulster Hall**
● **Ormeau Baths Gallery**

Below and Bottom: the Ormeau Baths Gallery

Map on page 20

Below: Belfast shops are designer-conscious
Bottom: eating out on Dublin Road

Amost unnoticed at the junction of Ormeau Avenue and Bedford Street, shaded under dusty trees, stands the **Thomas Thompson Memorial**, erected in memory of the founder of the city's Home for the Incurable. It takes the form of an elaborate crusty red Aberdeen granite and sandstone drinking fountain bearing the legend 'Who so drinketh of the water that I shall give him'. Thompson, a naval surgeon during the Napoleonic Wars, served in Latin America and the West Indies, gaining knowledge that enabled him to combat outbreaks of cholera, smallpox, dysentery and typhus in Belfast, not least during the Great Hunger of the 1840s when the potato crop failed.

Among the medieval-style heads carved below the spire of Thompson's fountain is one of the good doctor himself, sporting Dundreary whiskers and monocle. Since the fountain is now dry, perhaps a break is called for in **Morrison's Spirit Grocers** opposite, an entirely ersatz but enticing conglomeration of Edwardiana evoking an Ireland of the past, where beer engine and ham slicer – and often barber's razor and undertaker's wringing hands – were all wielded on the same premises.

DUBLIN ROAD

Along the **Dublin Road**, which runs south towards Shaftesbury Square, is a fairly concentrated stretch of (largely Asian) restaurants, pubs, fast-food joints, fashion shops and live music clubs, beginning with one of Belfast's largest cinema complexes, the multi-screen **Movie House** at No 14 (tel: 9075 3300). When the restaurants started burgeoning in the 1990s, locals

referred to the stretch as the Golden Mile, but the gold glisters less than it once seemed to.

Looking a little out of place, just down the road, is the impressive **Shaftesbury Square Reformed Presbyterian Church,** which dates from 1890.

A left turn from **Shaftesbury Square,** named after the 7th Earl of Shaftesbury, leads to a curious but rewarding blend of antiquity and motorbike salesrooms in **Donegall Pass,** the streets off it named after trees in the wood it once passed through. Here amidst walls of loyalist graffiti are several excellent antiques and fine arts shops and also some of Belfast's more interesting Chinese restaurants: the **Water Margin** in a converted church at the bottom of the road, and the atmospheric – and, for Belfast, unusually authentic – Chinese restaurant, **Sun Kee** (43–47 Donegall Pass).

SHAFTESBURY SQUARE

Shaftesbury Square itself is not particularly prepossessing but it does contain the popular Italian restaurant **Speranza**, behind a huge glass frontage and, behind a rather more arty print-embellished glass front, Paul Rankin's **Cayenne**, one of Belfast's top restaurants (on the site of his original trailblazing Roscoff).

High up on the **Ulster Bank**'s Portland stone at the corner of Dublin Road and Great Victoria Street there are also two of the best public art pieces in Northern Ireland. These floating **bronze figures ❽** by the sculptor Elizabeth Frink have been dubbed Draft and Overdraft by a public, who, with typical local humour, already called this end wall Clark's Gable after the Bank's then director.

GREAT VICTORIA STREET

Now proceeding north, the route follows **Great Victoria Street**, once an avenue of fine redbrick and stucco terraced houses. But the bombers of the 1970s continued what the planners had only in part achieved a decade earlier: the demotion of its southern half to a mix of car parks and brutal 1960s constructions. Now little but the ice cream-coloured stucco styling of the 1860s Great Victoria Street **Presbyterian Church** and the upper storeys of Victorian Richmond Terrace, north of the Ulster Bank, remain to tell of its former dignity.

Across the road is the entirely rebuilt **Apostolic Evangelical Pentecostal Church**, in the 1870s, the city's first synagogue. Vere Foster, the revolutionary education-

> **Dublin Road eateries**
> In a street packed with fast food outlets and short-lived ethnic restaurants, the glass-fronted Square (tel: 028 9023 9933), at No 89, stands out both for longevity and quality. On the other side of the road, Auntie Annie's Porterhouse (tel: 028 9050 1660), at No 44, typifies Belfast's growing reputation for unpretentious fun. With a strong live music component it's a great place to check out Belfast's upcoming bands.

Below: a facade on Great Victoria Street
Bottom: the Frink bronzes

Map on page 20

Opera House revival

Luciano Pavarotti made his UK debut in 1963 at the Grand Opera House, in Puccini's *Madame Butterfly*. Sarah Bernhardt, Orson Welles and Laurel and Hardy all appeared here. Thanks to a £9 million refurbishment in 2006, extended wing space means the historic venue (it opened in 1895) can now accommodate the biggest West End productions. There's also a bright, spacious new foyer, new restaurant and bars and an intimate new performance space, Baby Grand.

This bar in Great Victoria Street hosts traditional Irish music sessions

al philanthropist who helped many to America in the famine years of the 1840s, lived and died at No 115.

The polychrome brick building on the terrace's town side, **Shaftesbury Square Hospital**, designed by W. J. Barre in 1867, originally cared for those with ophthalmic problems and more latterly for those suffering another kind of darkness: substance abuse. Designed by Ian Campbell, Fanum House, grey, Lubianka-like, forbidding, stands to the north where Grattan & Co, in 1825, first manufactured aerated waters, founding an industry in which local firm Cantrell & Cochrane is still among the world's leaders.

Water was also a concern of the painter Paul Henry's father, minister at the **Great Victoria Street Baptist Church** on the corner of Hope Street. He scandalised his 1870 congregation by announcing he had lost faith in total-immersion baptism. The tiny house abutting is claimed as the city's narrowest. Henry senior would not have approved of the indulgence available at the award-winning Paul Stafford Beauty Salon next door.

On the other side of the road, **Days Hotel**, a huge modern building which apes the functional 1960s architecture that disfigured much of this area, makes up in value what its exterior lacks in aesthetic appeal.

GRAND OPERA HOUSE

The street's honeypot is the ★★★**Grand Opera House** ❾ (for Box Office and tours by arrangement, call 9024 1919). Designed by Frank Matcham, the theatre, on the corner of Glengall Street, is an oriental fantasy of minaret and pediment where even the ventilation lantern has a Moorish air to it. It hosts touring Shakespeares, opera, ballet, concerts of all kinds and post-West End musicals. Van Morrison's *Live at the Grand Opera House* was recorded there in 1984.

High on its frontage, a naked bronze Mercury takes flight and Shakespeare looks down approvingly. However, it is the interior which really delights, a riot of crimson and gold leaf with gilded elephant heads supporting the boxes and a heavenly ceiling mural added by Cherith, wife to Robert McKinstry, who carried out the major restoration of the building *(see margin note)*. Surprisingly, the theatre languished unloved as a cinema for much of the 1960s and was almost abandoned in the 1970s as a result of damage caused by a series of terrorist bombs.

This palace of varieties and delights is a little

dwarfed by the **Europa Hotel**, from whose comforts three decades of reporters covered the Troubles and which remains a key part of Belfast nightlife *(see Accommodation, page 126)*.

To its left, fronting the entrance to the Europa Bus-Centre and Rail Station, pose Louise Walsh's two clothed life-sized tributes to low-paid working women opposite Amelia Street, once the bordello area.

CROWN LIQUOR SALOON

Across the street, and linked (allegedly) by a tunnel allowing stage-door Johnnies to cozy chorus girls in its private snugs, is another riot of the Victorian Baroque, the ★★★**Crown Liquor Saloon ❿**, Belfast's most famous pub. Bought in 1978 by the National Trust (on the recommendation of Sir John Betjeman), it was once the Ulster Railway Hotel, dating from the same year as the Opera House, and was also restored by McKinstry.

It is a cream, three-storey stucco building whose ground-floor bar is lavishly tiled in many colours and whose snugs – with bronze match strikers and a bell that wags a flag to summon service – are guarded by griffin and lion. The superb tiling, glasswork and ornamental woodwork are the creation of Italian craftsmen, brought to Belfast in the 1880s to work on Catholic churches.

The ceiling is embossed, the oysters and Guinness admirable, the waiters amenable and the customers a mixed bunch of stage hands, actors, journalists, travel writers, students and open-mouthed tourists sometimes too overcome to call their order for a pint. Despite

Star Attractions
● **Grand Opera House**
● **Crown Liquor Saloon**

Below and Bottom: the Grand Opera House

Map
on page
20

Crowning glory

The Crown Liquor Saloon starred on the big screen when James Mason's haunted, hunted IRA man sought sanctuary in a perfect replica of the bar in Carol Reed's 1947 film noir classic *Odd Man Out*. The film, scripted from his own novel by the Belfast-based F. L. Green, conjures up a nightmarish, almost Dickensian vision of life in Belfast's back streets at that time.

moving into the modern marketing age, with website (www.crownbar.com) and live webcam, it remains one of the most authentic Victorian bars you can find.

That is not something that can be said for **Robinson's Bar**, two doors north, which was fire-bombed in 1991, gutting the interior, but has been rebuilt, its exterior faithfully, to the original 1846 design. It is now home to five bars, including the Irish themed Fibber Magee's, which opts for the full range of spirit grocer's artefacts and hosts traditional Irish music sessions. It also boasts the strikingly designed BT1 bar (named after Belfast's most fashionable post code) in the basement, plus, more recent additions, the Bistro restaurant/bar upstairs and, in the loft area, the Roxy, with live music and dance nights.

The **Beaten Docket**, named after a failed betting slip, is the jokey identity of the rather charmless and noisy Irish theme pub that faces the Crown across Amelia Street (although its interior is pure 1985).

PRESBYTERIAN ASSEMBLY ROOMS

Diagonally opposite from the Grand Opera House, across Fisherwick Place, is the rusticated sandstone Tudor Gothic bulk of the ★**Presbyterian Assembly Rooms** ⓫, the essential Englishness of its mullioned windows made dour by Scots corbelling and a crown spire copied from St Giles' Cathedral, Edinburgh. The doorway arch and oriel window above are carved with biblical burnishing bushes and 14 angels 'specially copied from life'. The contest for its design in 1899 was clouded in unbiblical scandal, however, the winner

*The Crown
Liquor Saloon.*

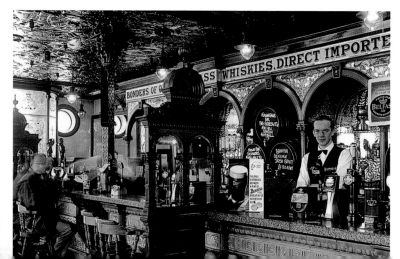

being the Church's own architect who devised the competition. The exterior turret clock was the first in these islands to use electricity to drive its cogs and to ring its 12-bell carillon of 28 tunes.

Now the ground floor is given over to an elegant shopping centre, the **Spires Mall** (tel: 9032 2284), with designer label shops and a café. The majestically polygonal Assembly Room upstairs, still one of the most impressive venues in Belfast, can be hired for conferences and concerts.

ROYAL BELFAST ACADEMICAL INSTITUTION

College Square takes its name from the fine square lawn that was to surround the Georgian symmetry of the long, three-storey dusky red brick of the ★★**Royal Belfast Academical Institution ⑫**, just north of Jury's Hotel opposite the Assembly Rooms. Now set beyond lawns much reduced, its spare elegance owing much to the 1807 designs by that great English architect Sir John Soane, it is the city's finest building. Belfast's first major centre of learning, the RBAI was set up to cater for all the major denominations of Christianity.

However, debts forced the governors to sell off land on which was built, in five storeys of Portland stone, the Municipal Technical Institute, now the **Belfast Institute** (a.k.a. the College of Knowledge). Its style is pompous Baroque Revivalist, its four copper domed turrets are impressive and the city's coat of arms is set above the main doorway.

But the loss of green sward, and the education of rude labourers, destroyed College Square East and North, and the square's cachet as *the* address for surgeons and academics – the physicist Lord Kelvin was born in No 17 East. The tall houses soon fell, first to commerce, then to the bomb.

Only the block containing, at No 7 College Square North, the **Old Museum** a Greek Revival building of the 1830s, attests to former glories. The Belfast Natural History Society, which still owns the place, engaged architect Thomas Jackson to erect this chaste building, modelling it on the Choragic Monument of Thrasyllus with its portico replicating that of Athens' tower of Andronicus and its upper portions the Temple of Minerva.

THEATRE AND ARTS CENTRE

Inside, is the ★**Old Museum Arts Centre ⑬**, (tel: 9023 3332) which has increasingly won a reputation

Below: ornamentation in the Crown Liquor Saloon
Bottom: the Presbyterian Assembly Rooms

Map
on page
20

The Black Man

This 1876 statue of rabble-rousing Presbyterian cleric, the Reverend Dr Henry Cooke, is not actually black but of green bronze. The original figure, curiously painted black and later moved to the City Hall, was of the 1885 Earl of Belfast. The reverend, whom Daniel O'Connell – 'The Liberator' to Nationalists in the mid-19th century – referred to as 'Bully Cooke', has his back turned to the Academy whose visionary notions on equality and radical science he desperately opposed.

for innovative dance, theatre and comedy at its compact 90-seat theatre and visual arts at its gallery. It's been an important sponsor of local talent too, with partnerships with local companies like Kabosh Theatre and Replay Productions. A move to a new £15 million arts venue in Talbot Street is scheduled for 2010.

Fans can only gaze across at the space where No 36 stood, serving originally as a Royal Irish Constabulary barracks, much later the Maritime Club where Van Morrison and Them first raised the roof with *G.L.O.R.I.A.*

The return to the Linen Hall Library is via Wellington Place, passing the '**Black Man**' on his plinth *(see margin note)*. An alternative approach to the Library is via the artists' studios of King's and Queen's streets, and then College Street, whose offshoot, **College Court**, was named Squeeze-Gut Entry in the 18th century.

The view north is of Cave Hill, its ridge profile dubbed Napoleon's Nose by citizens mocking the 1798 rebellion and cocking a snoot at the aggressive French emperor who had been persuaded to help drive the British out of Ireland.

WELLINGTON PLACE

Only Nos 7–11 of the original 1830 houses in **Wellington Place** remain. Named after the Duke of Wellington, who spent much of his boyhood at Annadale in the south of the city, this is a street of gift shops, fashion boutiques, cafés and music shops, which leads us back to our starting place, the Linen Hall Library.

The 'Black Man' statue of the Reverend Dr Henry Cooke

2: City Hall to Donegall Place

City Hall – conspirators' alleyways – High Street – Royal Avenue – Public Library – 1st Presbyterian Church – Queen's Arcade – Donegall Place

'Red brick on the gable/White Horse on the wall/Ital-i-an marble in the City Hall/Oh stranger from England, why look so aghast?/May the Lord in His Mercy look down on Belfast.' Thus wrote poet-architect Maurice James Craig, deftly summarising the one-time ethos of this city of redbrick terraces and politico-historical folk art ruled with sectarian despatch from inside the marbled halls of Sir Brumwell Thomas's 1906 wedding-cake **★★★City Hall ⓮** in Donegall Square (free guided tours at 11am, 2pm and 3pm Mon–Fri, and 2.30pm Sat, Jun–Sept and 11am and 2.30pm Mon–Fri and 2.30pm Sat, Oct–May. Special group tours may be booked in advance by calling 9027 0456).

The centre of Belfast life, both geographically and politically, the City Hall dominates the commercial heart of Belfast, imposing itself on the skyline from all angles, and is well worth investigating, not least for its magnificent interior. Conceived in response to Queen Victoria's award of city status to Belfast in 1888, building began in 1898 on the site of the former White Linen Hall, and took eight years to complete (amid criticism of its escalating costs, the final figure of around £360,000 was nearly twice the original budget).

By its centenary year in 2006, City Hall, once a symbol of unionist power, saw its Council Chamber occupied by an even mix of nationalist and unionist councillors, a result of the city's changing demographics.

City Hall will close for refurbishment from late 2007 for up to two years, though its grounds, a venue for events such as the Continental Markets, remain open.

A DEBT TO ST PAUL'S

The City Hall's design, freely appropriated from St Paul's Cathedral in London, has been dubbed 'Wren-aissance' but is deemed 'classical renaissance' by its admirers. Like a giant wedding cake, a verdigrised copper Ionic dome rises to 53m (173ft) above the centre. Two storeys of a 100-m (33-ft) Portland stone quadrangle, each corner equipped with a tower, surround a central courtyard.

In front stands Thomas Brock's statue of Queen Vic-

Below: the City Hall's 'Wrenaissance' exterior
Bottom: a Great Hall window

Map on page 20

The City Hall Gardens

The gardens are often used for public events, such as operas and concerts. Statues commemorate various worthies, from frock-coated mayors to James Magennis, who won his Victoria Cross in World II by placing mines from a midget submarine beneath an enemy boat. It was here in 1995 that President Bill Clinton addressed huge crowds during a hopeful phase of the peace process, near a single column of Portland stone recalling the first European touchdown of the US Expeditionary Force, who disembarked in Belfast on 26 January, 1942.

Inside the City Hall

toria, supported by a downtrodden but comely maiden spinning linen (the industry on whose wealth Belfast was largely built), a waif working material and a muscular shipwright's apprentice. Victoria's back is to the pedimented portico and its curious tomb-like portecochere, suggesting Her Majesty, not amused, has stepped out of her mausoleum.

In the gardens is a marble figure of Thane, also sculpted by Brock and erected to mark the sinking of that other icon of Belfast, the RMS *Titanic* in 1912.

Inside, an ornate carrara marble staircase sweeps up from the Pavonazzo and Brescia marble grandiloquence of the Entrance Hall to the Rotunda colonnaded in Cippalino marble. Off this are the Reception Room, Banqueting Hall and wainscoted Council Chamber laid out in Westminster House of Commons style.

Above the Rotunda, under the Great Dome, is the whispering gallery and John Luke's mural illustrating the foundation of the city and the industries that provided its wealth, commissioned to mark the 1951 Festival of Britain. The striking Great Hall (rebuilt after German bombing in 1941) has its original seven stained-glass windows, depicting three monarchs who have visited Belfast (King William III, Queen Victoria and King Edward VII) and the shields of Ireland's four provinces.

OSCAR WILDE'S CHOICE

Across **Donegall Square North**, turning right from the City Hall gates, the influence of Lanyon's firm crops up again in the red sandstone four-storey Venetian Gothic mass, completed in 1869 as a linen warehouse.

This later became the Water Office until magisterially restored by ★**Marks & Spencer ⑮**, the carved vegetable frieze quite suiting their business. On New Year's Day 1884, Oscar Wilde proclaimed this the city's sole beautiful building.

Taking its name from callendering, a smoothing process for linen, **Callender Street** was once an alleyway for the complementary businesses of distilling and newspaper publishing, now a short-cut through to pedestrianised **Castle Lane**. To the right, five streets converge on **Arthur Square**. There is fine Art Nouveau detailing on the 1906 Mayfair Building.

The 1870 ★**Masonic Building ⑯**, Nos 13–21, is by Lanyon's firm and stands on the site of oyster taverns, a trade that prospered down William Street South. Here in 1875, from still attractive Nos 13–19, William Ross planned wells 130m (420ft) deep to obtain pure water for his still extant and celebrated Belfast Ginger Ale. Centuries back, Donegalls moored their pleasure barges in what is now Arthur Street, and the Corn Market was what it says it was. Arthur Street is now moving upmarket, with designer label shops, **Habitat** and the sumptuous Parisian music hall-style **Café Vaudeville**, delightfully restored from an old bank.

ANN STREET

In **Ann Street**, around the corner, a traditional local business, boot-making, continues through a number of cut-price shoe shops. The street represents new times in Belfast, with the Glasgow Rangers shop just a few doors away from its Glasgow Celtic rival.

If you take the subway beneath Victoria Street to the final part of Ann Street you will find a touch of urban chic at **Mono**, a restaurant/bar at No 100 (tel: 9027 8886), with DJs Wednesday–Sunday and a classic French menu. Nearby, **Elliott's** has provided fancy dress and formal wear for over a century.

Before his execution, the 1798 Presbyterian leader Henry Joy McCracken was held in No 13 Ann Street when it served as the Artillery Barracks, before being hanged in the Corn Market. However, our interest lies in nipping in and out of the quarter's narrow pub-lined entries. From **Joy's Entry** in 1737 the revolutionary martyr's grandfather Francis Joy established what is now the oldest continuously published newspaper in the English language, the *Belfast News Letter*. The predecessor to its current rival, the *Irish News*, developed

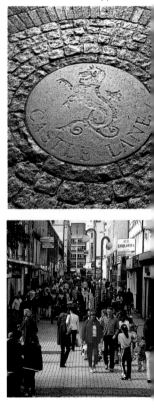

Below: paving in Castle Lane.
Below: Ann Street shoppers.

Map on page 20

The Pottingers
Pottinger's Entry is named after the family who supplied the city with gold sovereigns and the British army with moustached majors. The most noted of the family was Henry, who as Governor secured the British lease to Hong Kong after the Chinese Opium Wars.

*Below: the Morning Star
Bottom: keeping time at the city's leading newspaper*

from the *Morning News*, first published in 1853 at No 6 **Crown Entry**. The Society of United Irishmen was inaugurated in the Crown Tavern in 1791.

From **Wilson's Court** the first edition of the United Irishmen's own newspaper, the *Northern Star*, was published, and Belfast playwright Stewart Parker's play of the same name takes a sardonically sympathetic view of their editorial meetings. **Hamilton's Court** housed an 18th-century town sovereign. Born in a humble cooper's house in Cole's Entry, actress and courtesan Harriet Mellon rose to become Duchess of St Albans. The acclaimed landscape watercolourist and printmaker Andrew Nicholl (1804–86) was a bootmaker's son from **Church Lane**. Here, among the 18th and 19th-century houses, next to his old studio (now an Asian food shop), is a stylish bar and brasserie named for him. A few doors down, at No 4, is an atmospheric old tobacco shop, Miss Moran Ltd, named for the woman who owned it from the 1930s to 1980s.

Retracing our steps into Ann Street, we duck under a painted brick archway into **Pottinger's Entry**, past the distracting ambience of the ornate ★**Morning Star** ⑰ where Mary McCracken attempted to revive her brother, having first bribed the hangman. It is the last of the area's celebrated oyster houses. Still with its original facade and a wonderful old horseshoe bar, it was once a sailor's pub, situated at the start of the Dublin Coach route. Today, it's better known for its eclectic menu, which can include kangeroo, crocodile or emu steaks, courtesy of its Australian co-owner.

HIGH STREET

High Street takes the line of the Farset river which still flows beneath it. Here lived the McCracken family and Sir James Murray, patentor of Milk of Magnesia. To the left are **St George's Buildings**, three storeys of finely detailed stucco, behind which the city's first cinema opened in the Central Hall on 17 August 1908, packing in 1,500 for a showing of the silent movie *Bluebeard*.

Turning into Bridge Street, past a grey 1960s building housing an uninspiring shopping centre that, bafflingly, has been listed (nothing to do with the fact Murray once lived in a house on the site), you'll see the stylish ★**Northern Whig** pub ⑱ on the corner of Waring Street at what marks one entrance to the gradually developing Cathedral Quarter (*see Route 3, page 41*). Dating from 1819, the Northern Whig building has housed a hotel and newspaper offices (of the same name) and is now a Soviet-themed pub with chunky, comfortable furniture and a good all-day menu. A forerunner of the stylish bars that have pervaded Belfast, it remains one of its most enjoyable.

NORTH STREET

North Street, much redeveloped over recent decades, struggles to keep its once interesting character. You can find rare vinyl records at **Hector's House,** while anglers will enjoy **J Braddell and Son**, a highly respected fishing tackle and shooting shop is at No 11, nearby. Architecturally, the street's most interesting offering is, or perhaps was, the listed Art Deco **North Street Arcade**, linking North Street with Donegall Street in the Cathedral Quarter. The only example of a 1930s shopping arcade in Northern Ireland, with brass shop fronts and a terrazzo pavement, it was damaged by fire in 2004, believed by many to be an arson attack.

On the corner of Lower Garfield Street, stands the traditional Deer's Head pub, which still has five of its original Victorian snugs. At St Anne's Court, 59 North Street, the **Belfast and Northern Ireland Welcome Centre** *(see page 21)* deals with tourist information and bookings for anywhere in Northern Ireland.

BELFAST PUBLIC LIBRARY

Around the corner, into Royal Avenue, which has been the city's main shopping thoroughfare since Victorian times, is the French-looking three-storey ★**Belfast Public Library ⑲**, also in red sandstone, designed by

Below: North Street Arcade.
Bottom: Royal Avenue

Map on page 20

Below: Castle Court
Bottom: Smihfield Market

Lanyon's partner Lynn and completed in 1888. For those wishing to research Belfast or Northern Irish history and culture, this is as good a place as any to start, with a helpful staff, accessible and extensive collections and a wide range of periodicals and newspapers going back to the 19th century. Next door is the **Belfast Telegraph**, Northern Ireland's biggest-selling paper. Generally perceived as reflecting a moderate unionism, it is owned these days by a Catholic, Tony O'Reilly, as part of his Independent empire embracing newspapers in London, Dublin and South Africa.

Now the route turns on its head, to journey back down Royal Avenue towards Donegall Place and City Hall. The Albert, Gresham and Crown Chambers, on the right, retain some of their period charm, as do Donegall, Eagle, Royal and Avenue Chambers on the left. The reflective glass and stainless steel of **Castle-Court** shopping centre (tel: 9023 4591) reflects its confidence as the big hitter of the city-centre shopping centres (though this will change with the arrival of the Victoria Square retail development), with the likes of Debenhams, Dorothy Perkins, Miss Selfridge, Virgin Records and T.K. Maxx among its 70 retail outlets.

At the back of CastleCourt, in Winetavern Street, **Smithfield Market ⑳,** on the site of Belfast's famous Victorian market, has an interesting range of shops including comics, camping equipment, model soldiers and **Life Cycles**, (tel: 9043 9959), the best in Belfast for bike hire and guided cycle tours of the city.

Almost opposite the front of CastleCourt, at No 65 Royal Avenue, **Smyth's Irish Linen** is now Belfast's premier source for locally produced linen products such as tablecloths and napkins, as well as *Titanic* and Guinness merchandise.

Just further on, at No. 2, a largish Tesco Metro food store inhabits the old **Provincial Bank**, designed by W.J. Barre.

ROSEMARY STREET

Our route diverts east into **Rosemary Street** where Sarah Siddons, the celebrated actress, played its long-gone 18th-century Playhouse, just opposite the truly delightful **First** (Non-Subscribing) ★★**Presbyterian Church ㉑.** Dating from 1781, this is the city's oldest surviving place of worship. Its interior is boat-like and elliptical, its woodwork divine, its ceiling radially plastered, its pews boxed. Such was the fervour of dogma among 18th-century Dissenters that splits led them to build two further separate churches, since demolished, in the same street. In stark contrast, **Fresh Garbage**, at No 24 (tel: 9024 2350), is a longstanding treasure trove for those seeking alternative culture (from rock to hippy to punk), clothes, artefacts, and Celtic jewellery.

The route turns right into **Lombard Street**, from which the Irish Temperance League once operated, then smartly left again into the courtyard of **Winecellar Entry**, past the upturned cannon-barrel bollards to the atmospheric **White's Tavern**, associated with the wine trade since 1630 but much rebuilt.

A further right turn in this dingy canyon brings you back to High Street opposite Pottinger's Entry. Here the route continues left up High Street past the splendid Art Deco bulk of what was a 1930s Woolworth's and Burton's department store, standing on the site of the Market House from which, during the 1798 rebellion, corpses were hung out to rot.

CASTLE PLACE

Little remains in **Castle Place** that would suggest its former Victorian commercial focus as a place of silk merchants and tea shops and indeed of previous glories. The street furniture is ubiquitous and where Donegal Arcade (home to the excellent Irish gift shop, the **Wicker Man**) now runs was once the Provost Prison where those to be hanged from the Market House were held. On W. H. Lynn's five-storey red sandstone Bank Buildings, now **Primark**, the Victorian and Art Nouveau detail high up on the Woolwich at No 17 and

Star Attraction
● **First Presbyterian Church**

Before CastleCourt
When CastleCourt opened in 1985, it was hailed for the confidence of its investors in a city not yet, despite decades of commercial conflagration, at peace. Until the 1960s this was the site of the Grand Central Hotel, boasting Al Jolson, John McCormack and Paul Robeson among its guests. Later, when guests were understandably few, its once grand rooms were converted into a British Army base, housing colonels and squaddies, spies and double agents.

White's Tavern

Map on page 20

Robinson & Cleaver's
Originally a linen warehouse, this leading department store has six storeys, a clock tower, ogee copper domes, a flock of Donatello cherubs and 50 stone heads of those claimed as the firm's patrons, plus symbolic references to far-flung marketplaces. You can identify Queen Victoria, Prince Albert, George Washington and the man who first delineated the rules of snooker, the Maharaja of Cooch Behar.

Below: Kelly's Cellars
Bottom: Robinson & Cleaver's

Castle Buildings at Nos 8–18, gives a flavour of past times and glory.

Just right of the old Bank Buildings, **Bank Street** runs west to **Kelly's Cellars** ㉒, a public house established in 1720 and even today retaining some of the conspiratorial ambience generated when Henry Joy McCracken crouched beneath the counter escaping the Redcoats. A left turn takes us into **Chapel Lane**, past **St Mary's Roman Catholic Chapel**, whose walls date from 1783 and whose original opening was formally and ecumenically saluted by the Presbyterians of the 1st Belfast Volunteer Company.

Scruffy with black taxis and fruit and vegetable stalls, **Castle Street** is home to the 1865 Hercules Bar, and the Irish Tourist Board (Bord Fáilte). Queen Street has two excellent cafés, Café Renoir and Caffè Metz, some evangelical faith shops (Belfast hasn't completely changed) and some interesting arts and crafts shops.

Turn left into College Street, where there are a number of shops worthy of investigation. The **Bradbury Art Gallery** (3 Lyndon Court, tel: 9023 3535) has regular exhibitions of contemporary art, numerous special events and a well-stocked shop next door.

FOUNTAINS CENTRE

Outside the **Fountains Centre**, almost opposite, a remarkable automated musical clock strikes the hour with a curious procession of characters from Alice in Wonderland and the Nativity. Within are a branch of Smyth's Irish Linens and Utopia, a gift shop with striking Italian chess sets, traditional Russian lacquer dolls and much else. Nearby, Sawers is a traditional Belfast deli with excellent local fish and seafood delicacies (like potted herring and smoked Irish wild salmon) and Irish cheeses, while Global Creations sells fair trade clothes and gifts from the developing world.

Café Altos, Café Rankin and the Fountain Bar are worth a mention in Fountain Street, from which the 1880s-built ★**Queen's Arcade** ㉓, now largely inhabited by jewellery and watch shops, leads us back on to **Donegall Place**, now colonised almost entirely by British high-street multiples.

Above **Queen's Arcade Buildings** is a Disneyesque maquette of Belfast Castle. On the other side of Donegall Place stands what was once the province's leading store, still bearing the name, high up, of **Robinson & Cleaver's** ㉔ *(see margin note).*

3: The Cathedral Quarter

**The Exchange – Northern Ireland War Memorial –
Hill Street – Belfast Community Circus – St Anne's
Cathedral – John Hewitt pub – The Kremlin –
Irish News – Saint Patrick's Church**

The opening of the luxurious new Merchant Hotel in
2006 gave a massive impetus to Belfast's much vaunt-
ed new cultural area, the Cathedral Quarter, named
after its most significant landmark, St Anne's Cathedral. Along with a new arts venue, the Black Box, the
Merchant, which has a pub and club attached, has
become the hub of a thriving social scene. The area is
still some way off achieving parity with districts such
as Dublin's Temple Bar, the ultimate aim of the regeneration project, but there is now more than enough to
enjoy here to make a special tour worthwhile. This
most historic part of Belfast, located between the city-
centre and waterfront, has been home to revolutionaries, bohemians, visiting sailors, and least socially
respectable of all, journalists, for over two centuries.

*Below: festival time in the
Cathedral Quarter
Bottom: appreciative audience
for street performers*

ENTERTAINMENTS CENTRE

By the 1990s, much of the area had fallen into disre-
pair and, given that a good proportion of its Victorian
warehouses and offices still remained, it was considered the best location to create the kind of mixed artistic, commercial and entertainment district that had
made the likes of Temple Bar so successful. The now
defunct Laganside Corporation, having already

Map
on page
20

The Demon Drink

Belfast's population explosion in the 18th century meant that, by the time Queen Victoria came to the throne in 1836, there were 346 public houses, many offering accommodation and, later, musical entertainment. According to one count, Barrack Street, off Divis Street, had 53 businesses, of which 15 were pubs. The vicissitudes of the city's taverns are recounted in *Historic Pubs of Belfast* by Gary Law, published by Appletree Press.

Live traditional Irish music is a regular feature in many bars

achieved the transformation of Belfast's waterfront, was given the task of overseeing the redevelopment some years ago.

Much of its success in establishing a cultural identity has been down to a very well-regarded alternative annual arts festival, the Cathedral Quarter Arts Festival, (www.cqaf.com) which, in April or May, brings a wide variety of Irish and international artists to venues throughout the quarter. Apart from various artistic galleries and workshops, media groups, a circus school, and several cutting-edge bars and night clubs, the area has also been claimed by Belfast's increasingly confident gay and lesbian population, whose own festival, Belfast Pride, grows bigger each year *(see page 47)*.

OUTSTANDING ARCHITECTURE

We begin the route where Bridge Street meets Waring Street. Opposite the popular Northern Whig pub *(see page 118)*, is another excellent building, the original 1769 **Exchange,** converted to a bank, the Northern, by Lanyon in 1845. Italianate stucco, the architect's trademark, is everywhere. All mileage from Belfast was calculated from here and in 1792 the premises hosted the famous Harp Festival, during which the young musicologist Edward Bunting transcribed the traditional airs and compositions of the last of this island's blind harpers.

Across Donegall Street, the lovely facade of the **Four Corners** building has been preserved and the building will become a Tulip Inn hotel in 2008. The **Northern Ireland War Memorial Building ㉕** (Mon–Fri 9am–5pm, free), at Nos 9–13 Waring Street has a permanent exhibition on Northern Ireland in the Second World War, including contemporary newspapers, photographs and letters.

The **Royal Ulster Rifles Museum** (5 Waring Street, tel: 9033 2086) traces the regiment back to 1793.

Just off Waring Street, a slight detour to Skipper Street (named as such as it provided lodging for tea clipper skippers) brings us to (at what was once the Opium nightclub) **The Spaniard,** at no 3 (tel: 9023 2448), which offers wine and tapas.

Further down, the recently refurbished **Nest** at Nos 22–28 (tel: 9024 5558) is part of Belfast's gay scene.

Walking back to Waring Street, on the corner is the **Ulster Buildings**, a solid 1869 sandstone block opposite the startling cubic frontage of the three-storey

Potthouse, (tel: 9024 4044), actually at No One Hill Street, though it faces onto Waring Street. Built on the site of a 17th-century potthouse, a history reflected in the use of materials – stone, wood, glass and cobblestones – to construct the new building (circa 2004). Inside are the Potthouse bar and grill, with food more comfort than chic, leading to a small, but, in summer, highly prized patio, with the Sugar Room nightclub, and a private party room, Soap, upstairs.

This was once the site of William Waring's home, a tanner for whom the street was named. His daughter, Jane, grew up to become Dean Jonathan Swift's *Varina*, refusing to marry him while he was prebendary at Kilroot, near Carrickfergus, in 1696.

Next door to the Potthouse, **Cotton Court** at Nos 30–42, an old bonded warehouse, is one of three managed workspaces in the area. It's home to an eclectic mix, including the **Belfast Print Workshop** (tel: 9023 1323), which provides facilities for artists who work in the various printmaking media, from etching and lithography to relief printing and screen printing. It also has Northern Ireland's first original print gallery and shop. Cotton Court also houses Craft NI and the Vision arts and crafts gallery.

FROM BANKING TO BEDS

The street's final building of distinction is the delightful 1860s **Ulster Bank** building, now the **Merchant Hotel** ㉖ with its elaborate cast-iron balustrade and extravaganza of Thomas Fitzpatrick's carvings. The skyline is dominated by his figures of Britannia, Justice and

Star Attraction
● **Merchant Hotel**

Below and Bottom: the former Ulster Bank, now the Merchant Hotel, and its carvings

Map on page 20

The Merchant Hotel

Like the bank it used to be, the hotel radiates wealth, not least in the spectacular Great Room restaurant where Ireland's largest chandelier hangs beneath a glass cupola. Its 21 lavishly decorated rooms and 5 suites named after Irish writers such as C.S. Lewis (prices from £220 to £600 a night), the New York-style Cloth Ear pub and opulent Ollie's nightclub add up to Belfast's most luxurious hotel. Naturally, a chauffeur-driven Bentley Arnage is available. *See listing, page 126.*

A gargoyle entertains during the Festival of Fools, Ireland's only international street theatre festival

Commerce. Urns surmount the corners. The Grade A listed building was bought for £1.8 million by Beannchor, which runs various Belfast restaurants and bars such as TaTu. Having spent £10 million on restoring it, the company relaunched it in 2006 as the luxurious Merchant Hotel, intended to compare favourably with the best that London has to offer *(see margin box)*.

Paved with setts and with its many hidden courtyards, entries (their corners protected from carriage wheels by heavy iron bollards) and listed brick and stucco warehouses, the cobblestoned **Hill Street** typifies the promise that earned the area its regeneration. At Nos 18–22 the new **Black Box** auditorium (tel: 9024 4400) hosts drama, comedy, cabaret and music.

Once a bonded warehouse, built for the famous Bushmills Whiskey Company, dating from 1832, **Nick's Warehouse ㉗** at Nos 35–39 (tel: 9043 9690) has been a major player on the Belfast eating scene since 1989 *(see page 113)*. Opposite Nick's is the popular **Hill Street Brasserie**.

FESTIVAL OF FOOLS

Just off Hill Street, Gordon Street has one of the quarter's more unusual stars, the **Belfast Community Circus** at Nos 23–25 (tel: 9023 6007), located here since 1999. Visitors can participate in evening classes on Wednesdays, or less energetically, simply watch their accomplished performers throughout the year, from special days at St Georges Market to numerous City Council events.

Biggest of all is their own **Festival of Fools**, usually held as part of the Cathedral Quarter festival in April/May, with trapeze artistes, jugglers, clowns, acrobats and wirewalkers in action on the area's streets.

ST ANNE'S CATHEDRAL

A left turn leads to largely demolished Talbot Street (which will be part of a big redevelopment project in the immediate area) running alongside the Protestant **★★St Anne's Cathedral ㉘**, a neo-Romanesque construction of Portland stone begun in 1898 and still lacking a spire (though this is to be belatedly rectified, after a design for a spire was chosen by the Cathedral board in October 2005). It succeeds a previous Parish Church, named as much after Anne, wife of the fifth Earl of Donegall, as Mary's mother.

The rather plain nave's spaciousness is due in part to it being built around its predecessor, where services were held until 1903. The pulpit, designed by Gilbert Scott, was carved by Harry Hems. Impressive features include a tympanum filled with a mosaic of angel musicians on a background of gold, one of Ireland's largest church organs, and delightful stained-glass windows. The baptistry contains a ceiling made of 150,000 pieces of glass, representing the basic elements of creation.

If we now turn left and walk to the beginning of Donegall Street, we can explore the part of the street we missed while walking down Hill Street, before proceeding northwards again. Exchange Place at No 23, houses **Belfast Exposed** (tel: 9023 0965), Northern Ireland's only dedicated photographic gallery, which has a large archive of digital images.

ARTS ENTERPRISES

Exchange Place also includes the offices of the **Belfast Film Festival** (tel: 9032 5913, www.belfastfilmfestival.org), which usually takes place in April, with a programme of premieres, classics and short film competitions. Their Visions Studio also has a programme of digital screenings through the year. **Northern Visions** community media arts centre, which helps local film and video makers, is also here (tel: 9024 5495).

At No 25, **Open Windows Productions** (tel: 9032 9669) offers a trinity of exotic chess sets, courtesy of sculptor Anto Brennan. He's followed the success of his peace process set (an example of which sits in McHughs pub on the waterfront), featuring Gerry

Star Attraction
● **St Anne's Cathedral**

Below and Bottom:
St Anne's Cathedral,
interior and exterior

Map
on page
20

Below: the Duke of York
Bottom: drag artist Baroness
Titty Von Tramp performs on
the bonnet of an RUC Saracen
when a bomb scare disrupted
the opening evening of the
Kremlin nightclub

Adams, Paisley *et al*, with a Middle East set with Osama Bin Laden lining up opposite George Bush and a set based on RMS *Titanic*. He also sells models, prints, and portraits.

Just off Donegall Street, in Commercial Court, **The Duke of York** was a hacks' pub where Gerry Adams, President of Sinn Féin, worked as a barman in the 1960s. Today it's better known for a strong roster of live music through the week. Nearby is **Printers**, a café and wine bar with the area's best sandwiches.

One of Belfast's most culturally lively pubs, the community-run **John Hewitt** (named for a famous local poet), is at No 51. Though a relatively recent addition to the area it has an atmospheric traditional feel. Food is of a high gastropub standard, and the music, traditional, jazz and blues, is excellent. It's also a hub of activity during festival time.

We pass St Anne's again, perhaps delaying opposite the Cathedral, where the new Writers' Square contains diverting sculptural pieces by John Kindness and Brian Connolly and, during the festival, a large marquee for musical and comedy events.

ACADEMY STREET

Right off Donegall Street is **Academy Street**, so called after David Manson's 1768 co-educational establishment. Despite regulations forbidding dogs and guns, nine pupils at No 2, now demolished but once the Belfast Academy, took their masters hostage at gunpoint when they heard Easter Holidays were to be cancelled. No 40, built as a distiller's warehouse,

now houses the Belfast Education and Library Board. Across from the pleasing facade of the 1901 Cathedral Buildings, the £35 million redevelopment of the **Ulster University Art School** will be completed in 2008.

GAY BELFAST

Back on Donegall Street, over Royal Avenue, at No 96, is the **Kremlin**, (tel: 9031 6060) a soviet-themed nightclub which, with its sister and adjoining outfit, the **Union Street Bar and restaurant** (8–14 Union Street, tel: 9031 6060), forms the hub of Belfast's increasingly visible gay and lesbian scene, alongside the aforementioned Nest and the Mynt, on the outer edges of the Cathedral Quarter at 2–16 Dunbar Street, tel: 9023 4520. There's also a newcomer, **DuBarry's** (10–14 Gresham Street, tel: 9032 3590).

Despite vocal opposition from the Rev. Ian Paisley's Free Presbyterians, the Belfast Pride Festival celebrates this new confidence with a week of parties, concerts, talks, discos, and a parade around the city-centre, usually in late July or early August.

Near the Kremlin and opposite the *Irish News* is a journalist's pub with the giveaway name of **The Front Page**. Family-run, it's now best known as a leading venue for live local rock music. The adjoining frontage is a pleasant 1932 reconstruction of the German blitz-damaged 1860 sandstone of **Donegall Street Congregational Church**.

ST PATRICK'S

John Willis, first organist at the 1815 Gothic Revivalist **★★Saint Patrick's** Roman Catholic Church ㉙ beyond, was dismissed almost as soon as he was engaged for playing variations on *The Boyne Water*, a belligerent Orange Protestant marching tune, at a service. The side chapel triptych of St Patrick, the Madonna and St Bridget is by the society painter and war artist Sir John Lavery (who had been baptised in the church). The Madonna's face is that of Lavery's wife Hazel, said by her husband to have influenced her friend, Irish revolutionary Michael Collins, to sign the Anglo Irish treaty of 1921 that issued in partition.

Next to the church, Saint Patrick's School is of an even earlier vintage (1828). The elegant three-storey houses north, from 1796 or 1820, have recently been restored, making them, either way, among the earliest block of domestic premises to survive in the city.

Star Attraction
● St Patrick's RC Church

> **Funding St Patrick's**
> In the early 19th century Roman Catholics accounted for around one-sixth of Belfast's population and their numbers were growing to cater for the demands of new industries. A new church was needed, and a plot of ground was leased in 1809 from the Marquis of Donegall. Of the £4,100 raised to finance St Patrick's construction, £1,300 was subscribed by Protestants – an indication that the two communities were not always at each others' throats.

St Patrick at his church

4: Queen's Quarter

Crescent Arts Centre – Crescent Gardens – Queen's University – Elmwood Hall – Ulster Museum – Botanic Gardens – Botanic Avenue

An elegant area, one of Belfast's more rewarding for lovers of Victorian and Edwardian architecture, Queen's Quarter also has lively student pubs and stylish bars, many of the city's ethnic restaurants, art galleries, boutique hotels and budget hostels and Belfast's best known road for fashion hunting. The autumnal Belfast Festival at Queen's, which is centred around the area, is the second biggest arts festival in the UK after Edinburgh and makes an excellent introduction to the city for the first-time visitor as it utilises so many venues around Belfast.

BRADBURY PLACE

During the 1950s and 1960s, ★**Lavery's Gin Palace** ❸⓿ at 12–16 Bradbury Place, just south of Shaftesbury Square, was a haven for artists and poets including William Conor, John Hewitt and Louis MacNeice. It is also one of the few bars where town still meets gown and offers a wide range of live music throughout the week, from reggae to folk.

Also in Bradbury Place is a mix of fast-food restaurants of various kinds. **Bishop's** is a tiled haven of traditional fish 'n' chips (some say the best in Belfast), while the name of the nearby all-you-can-eat buffet noodle bar **Foo Kin**, at No 38, indicates its high student appeal. Across the road is the **M-Club**, at Nos 23–31 (tel: 9023 3131) a very popular dance venue which operates dance nights and parties on Thursdays, Fridays and Saturdays and has a strong student following.

At Nos 7–21, **Benedict's Hotel** (tel: 9059 1999), is a three-star boutique hotel with a popular bar, usually with live music until the early hours, and a restaurant.

Further south, past No 48's octagonal Art Deco weathercock-topped gazebo and over the railway bridge, into the **University Conservation Area**, there stands at the corner of University Road and Lower Crescent the 1873 Scrabo stone Scots baronial pile that is the ★**Crescent Arts Centre** ❸❶ (tel: 9024 2338). This maze of rooms and studios is noted for its devotion to New Age diversions, Latin American gigs, eclectic theatre and the excellent contemporary **Fendersky art gallery** and is always worth checking out. The centre also runs

Map
on page
49

Lisburn Road

A lengthy detour from Bradbury Place, taking the right fork along the long Lisburn Road, will take dedicated followers of fashion to a series of designer label boutiques and accessories shops, interspersed with gourmet deli/cafés and a host of art galleries. Worth checking out is Tom Caldwell (No 429, tel: 028 9066 1890), who continues a longstanding family tradition, combining a large selection of contemporary furniture and an art gallery, which has exhibited most of Ireland's finest artists over nearly four decades. Café Milano, Shu and Ta Tu are all elegant fixtures on the eating scene *(see pages 113–4)*. Once asking for Cambozola Brie and strawberries at a sandwich shop in Belfast would have met with the blankest of stares. Now it's a standard item on the menu at Doorsteps (Nos 445–457, tel: 028 9068 1645), which is one of the city's best, as lunchtime queues testify.

The Crescent Arts Centre

Belfast's major literary festival, *Between the Lines,* each spring, a midsummer dance festival and regular workshops and classes in all aspects of the arts. A multimillion pound refurbishment and extension got under way in late 2007.

Across University Road is tiny **King William Park**, commemorated in Frank Ormsby's ironic poem of the same name, where William III hitched his horse in 1690. Its southern neighbours are topped by the pinnacled spire of the 1887 **Moravian church** and the campanile of the **Wesleyan chapel**, designed by W. J. Barre, which would not look out of place in Lombardy. The Crescent Centre's neighbour is the **Crescent Church**, charismatic in its worship, French medieval in its architectural inspiration, God's light shining through its pierced campanile.

The Crescent Church

BARS AND BRASSERIES

Our route nips east behind the church past the grand pilasters of the stuccoed Georgian terraces of **Lower Crescent** and the pleasant **Crescent Gardens** ❸❷ (once a potato patch), perhaps stopping for a pint at the quirkily designed **Fly**, one of the earlier, and more striking, of the stylish bars that have cropped up around Belfast.

A little further on is one of the city's earliest boutique hotels, the three–star **Crescent Townhouse** (No 13, tel: 9032 3349) a 19th-century building whose suites are bathed in Ralph Lauren period decor. Adjoining are its **Bar Twelve** and **Metro** brasserie, both popular.

Returning to join imposing Upper Crescent and then University Road, we pass southwards to the pleasant stucco and Doric porticos of **Mount Charles**, once home to the novelist Forrest Reid and the poet John Hewitt.

Along University Road are a number of restaurants, ranging from the ever-popular **Villa Italia**, through a branch of the world-dominating rib specialist **Tony Roma's** to local favourite **Beatrice Kennedy's** (see Dining). **The Globe** bar at No 36 is

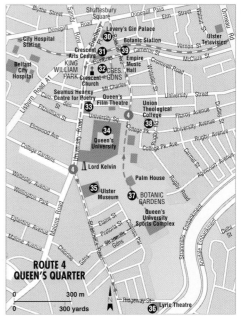

ROUTE 4
QUEEN'S QUARTER

0   300 m

0   300 yards

Map on page 49

The University

Queen's University's campus is modest in size and so, as the university expanded to its present 24,000 students and 1,600 teaching and research staff, it began buying up every vacant building in the area. Currently it owns more than 250 buildings. A large proportion of students come from Northern Ireland and, as many of those with families outside Belfast travel home at weekends, social activities at weekends are less extensive than one might expect.

The Great Hall at Queen's University

also popular, not least with karaoke aficionados. Across the road are three Georgian rows, Prospect Terrace, Botanic View and Cinnamond's Buildings, plus the Victorian stucco and Georgian brick terraces of Camden and Fitzwilliam Streets. These, respectively, were home ground for Brian Moore's 1956 novel *The Lonely Passion of Judith Hearne* and Nobel Laureate poet Seamus Heaney's campus flat.

The bookish may wish to dawdle over a tortilla and coffee while flicking through one of an excellent selection of secondhand books at the small but atmospheric **Bookfinder's Café** at No 47 (tel: 9032 8269).

Next comes Georgian **University Square** where several houses – now university departments – sport magnolia in their gardens. The Church of Ireland's Canon Hannay (1865–1950) a.k.a. George A. Birmingham, the nationalistic author of 60-plus satirical novels, lived at No. 75 University Road. The painter Paul Henry lived at No. 61. At No. 1 is the new ★**Seamus Heaney Centre for Poetry** ❸ (tel: 9097 1070), attached to the School of English at Queen's and a fairly regular venue for literary talks and events of a consistently high calibre. At No 20 University Square is the **Queen's Film Theatre**, the best place (actually, the only place) to catch the latest in world cinema in Belfast (tel: 9097 1097; www.queensfilmtheatre.com). It has two big screens, a theatre and a comfortable bar and lounge in which to debate the relative merits of Yasujiro Ozu and Quentin Tarantino.

QUEEN'S UNIVERSITY

Charles Lanyon designed the pleasingly mellowed dusty redbrick facade of ★★★**Queen's University** ❸, shamelessly appropriating the lines of the Founder's Tower at Magdalen College, Oxford, for its central feature. The university was first named Queen's College after the young Victoria when she laid the foundation stone in 1845. As suited the hierarchical nature of the times, the architect provided lavish accommodations for Chancellors and other dignitaries while offering the students little except four water closets and a row of urinals. Happily, this is now compensated by a new off-campus student village, the Elms, whose accommodation can be booked by visitors in the summer (*see page 127*).

There are over 100 listed buildings, dating back as far as 150 years, around the campus and surrounding area and it's worth buying the *Queen's Architectural Heritage Trail* booklet from the Visitor Centre (tel: 9097

5252) to help you on a signposted tour. In particular, search out at the Great Hall, which Lanyon based on the medieval great halls of the Oxbridge universities.

Also check out the **Naughton Gallery** in the Lanyon Building, which houses the university's own collection and often hosts interesting touring exhibitions. The post-war **Sir William Whitla Hall**, is regular concert venue.

Opposite the University's lawns stands its grim Student's Union (which houses one of the city's most popular dance clubs, **Shine**, founded in 1995) and the delightful Italianate deconsecrated wedding cake, **Elmwood Hall**, home to the acclaimed Ulster Orchestra. Above its three-tiered Presbyterian spire a gilt weathercock catches the sun. The **University Bookshop** adjoins. Further down Elmwood Avenue is a Non-Subscribing Presbyterian spire and what is now the Catholic Chaplaincy, where the poet Philip Larkin wrote many of his finest lines.

South of the University, past Methodist College on the right, the road divides into Malone and Stranmillis, the former a middle-class expanse of leafy avenues. Stranmillis Road, by contrast, has an off-campus feel to it, so our route left enters the gates of the Botanic Gardens *(see page 52)* by its 1912 statue to Lord Kelvin, formulator of the Second Law of Thermodynamics. Students are rude about his two accompanying metal spheres.

ULSTER MUSEUM

To the right, through the fir trees of the sombre pinetum, is the splendid ★★★**Ulster Museum** ❸ (tel: 9038 3000, open Mon–Fri 10am–5pm, Sat 1–5pm, Sun 2–5pm; admission free), once the municipal Art Gallery. Now

Star Attractions
● **Queen's University**
● **Ulster Museum**

Below: Elmwood Hall
Bottom: Queen's University

Map
on page
49

The Lyric's future
Although not built on a major scale, the Lyric, founded by Mary and Pearse O'Malley in 1951, has produced some of the finest drama to come out of Northern Ireland. Liam Neeson played here in Brian Friel's *Philadelphia, Here I Come!* in 1976. The sum of £12 million has been set aside to build a new 400-seat theatre and 150-seat studio space on the existing site, hopefully by 2009.

The Ulster Museum: exterior and a display of mummies

Belfast's industrial heritage and Irish history and art, from earliest civilisation to modern times, join a wealth of permanent and travelling exhibitions. Other floors concentrate on the island's biological, geological, and social heritages.

One of the best collections of Irish art from the 17th century onwards, as well as British and European paintings from the same period can be found at the excellent art gallery. Always popular are the artefacts rescued from the Spanish Armada galleass *Gerona*, sunk off the north coast in 1588, as well as Princess Takabuti, the first mummy to be displayed outside Egypt, known as Belfast's oldest bleached blonde due to her chemically discoloured hair. The museum also offers regular backpacks and trails for children, as well as lectures, master classes and occasional musical evenings.

Note that the museum will be closed until 2009 for extensive renovations.

Leaving the museum, go uphill past the cholera mound and Victorian angels of Friar's Bush Cemetery, dating not from a spurious 483AD tombstone but from a 16th-century friary. Away to the left are views of the white bulk of Stormont on distant hills, ahead the bistros and hair snippers of Stranmillis village, one of the most charming parts of Belfast. It also has one of the city's most important cultural outlets, the **Lyric Theatre** ㊱ (55 Ridgeway Street, tel: 9038 1081), where film star Liam Neeson first trod the boards *(see margin note)*.

BOTANIC GARDENS

Stranmillis Gardens leads back into ★★★**Botanic Gardens** ㊲ (open daylight hours) where a northwestern course through roses and hedged walks sets fair for both ★**Tropical Ravine** and ★★**Palm House**. In the 1889 Ravine, water drips from banana leaves in a miniature sunken rainforest while palm fronds form exotic patterns against the glass dome of the Palm House, executed 50 years earlier (and before he built the Great Palm House at Kew Gardens) by iron-founder Richard Turner to Lanyon's designs. Much enjoyed by students on sunny days, the Gardens are a regular venue for opera and rock concerts, like the annual Tennent's Vital Festival which attracts top names each summer. Other annual events include Belfast's Indian festival, Mela and Garden Gourmet, a celebration of food and flowers.

Beyond the Palm House the north gate leads on to College Park and Botanic Avenue, while an optional diversion via the east gate takes you first through a district of neat red-brick terraces and a profligacy of churches known as the **Holy Land** because so many of its street names derive from biblical cities. Padraic Fiacc's poems have their homes here.

Ahead is the formidable Scrabo stone mass of the ★**Union Theological College** ❸, its colonnaded facade *(pictured on page 107)* by Lanyon. Persuasive charm gains entry to the impressive colonnaded and domed **library**, used by Northern Ireland's House of Commons while it awaited Stormont's completion. Its Senate sat in the chapel.

Star Attraction
● **Botanic Gardens**

BOTANIC AVENUE

The houses of Botanic Avenue retain, on their 2nd and 3rd floors, evidence of their 1870s origins. Deemed Belfast's *Boul' Mich'* (Boulevard St Michel in Paris) by Seamus Heaney, it now carries itself with a raffish louche air, its tree-lined pavements fronting on to bookmakers, bookshops and brasseries, B&Bs and coffee bars.

Worth checking out here are **Café Renoir**, whose delicious pizzas come from a wood-fired oven, the stylish **AM:PM** café bar, **Dukes Hotel,** the crime-specialist bookshop, **No Alibis**, the jovial Italian restaurant **Scalini** (replete with Romeo and Juliet balcony), and **Madison's Hotel** with its eye-catching frontage.

The atmospheric **Empire Music Hall** ❸ (tel: 9032 8110) – in a deconsecrated church – provides live music and excellent stand-up comedy (in university term time) as well as a lively bar. Past Kingham Mission Church, and you are back at Shaftesbury Square.

Botanic Gardens: open-air concert and Palm House

Map on page 20

The Shipbuilding Era

In the early years of the 20th century, 17 percent of UK tonnage was being built by the Belfast yards of Harland & Wolff and Workman & Clark. More than 20,000 men were employed – the aristocrats of Belfast's working class. Even then, decades before Northern Ireland was created, six out of seven workers were Protestant, and networks of family and friends made sure that apprenticeships for the best-paid skilled jobs went to Protestants.

The Titanic Memorial

5: Titanic Quarter

Titanic Memorial – St George's Market – Belfast Waterfront Hall – Courts – Albert Memorial Clock – Custom House – Harbour Office – Sinclair Seamen's Presbyterian Church – Clarendon Dock – Odyssey – St George's Church

There are those among the more sceptical locals who question the wisdom of Belfast identifying itself ever more closely with a ship largely famous for sinking on its maiden voyage. Such voices of dissent carry little weight these days. A major annual festival, **Titanic – Made in Belfast**, is now firmly established on the city's calendar of events every April, and there is a £1 billion development of a small city of apartments, hotels, restaurants, bars and science park, plus a proposed £100 million *Titanic* visitor attraction, on 185 acres of the former shipyard where the legendary liner was built.

Despite its watery fate in 1912, *Titanic* was a remarkable creation – innovative, superbly crafted and built on an extraordinary scale. It was, in other words, an appropriate and easily identifiable symbol of Belfast's past pre-eminence as a shipbuilder. By the time City Hall was built in 1906, the city was not only one of the world's greatest ports but also a world leader in rope making, tobacco and other industries. *Titanic* was thus built at the apex of Belfast's ambition, belief and sense of self-importance – qualities many wish to see revived in post-peace process Belfast. Those wishing to know more about RMS *Titanic* should visit the website of the Belfast Titanic Society (prime movers of the Titanic festival) at www.belfast-titanic.com.

Strictly speaking, the recently designated Titanic Quarter alludes to the massive new development on the former Harland and Wolff shipyard, including the Odyssey complex which adjoins it, but a *Titanic* theme sits comfortably with this broader route.

Starting in the grounds east of the **City Hall,** at the base of the ★**Titanic Memorial ④**, two weeping sea-nymphs break the sea's cold grasp at the feet of a scantily clad marble statue of a female Fame, in their arms the *Titanic*'s *Unknown Soldier*, an anonymous drowned man. An inscription in gold leaf records the names, including that of Andrews, of just 11 'gallant Belfast men who lost their lives on 15 April 1912 by the foundering of the Belfast-built *Titanic* through collision with an iceberg, on her maiden voyage from Southampton to New York'. But there is no mention of the dozens of doomed Belfast-born artisan crew and steerage-class passengers – or indeed of any women – on board. The 11 gallants comprised the shipyard's Guarantee Group, who were checking performance targets on the vessel's maiden voyage.

Nearby, an aggressive bronze figure in topee and puttees serves as an 1899–1902 **Boer War** cenotaph. The rock on which he stands is, as was the custom of the times, supported by two bare-breasted and two flimsily covered goddesses with pert *embonpoint*.

Opposite, at Nos 11–13 Donegall Square East, is a hexastyle Corinthian porticoed facade which is all that remains of the original once-grand 1840s **Methodist Church**. Its congregation long gone to the suburbs, its dull 1,500-seat auditorium transferred from God to Mammon and its fine box pews cannibalised for pubs and restaurants, it has been rebuilt as the Ulster Bank's corporate HQ. Harry Ferguson designed the minimal-maintenance Ferguson tractor, revolutionising British farming, at Nos 14–16. Other 19th-century shipbuilders lived at Nos 18–20.

MAY STREET

The rabble-rousing Reverend Henry Cooke preached in May Street's 1859 classically designed **Presbyterian Church** ⑪. It was, after all, built as a vehicle large enough to accommodate both his ego and his 1,700-strong congregation. Nevertheless, it refused Temperance meetings and gave serious consideration to a pro-

Below: the Titanic's designer, Thomas Andrews, who went down with the ship
Middle: the Titanic sets sail
Bottom: the annual Titanic – Made in Belfast exhibition

Map on page 20

Sovereigns of the city

May Street takes its name from the May family who curried society's favours, marrying Anna, an illegitimate daughter, to the second Marquis of Donegall. Although they became sovereigns of the city, the callous, snobbish marquis kept the marriage secret. A great linen warehouse by Lanyon once stood at the top of the street on the right, and another Lanyon creation, originally the Church of Ireland Diocesan Offices, in polychrome brick, still stands opposite. Each December, the May Street Choir sings carols by candlelight in period dress around the area.

St George's Market

posal to use its basement cemetery as a bonded whiskey warehouse. Inside there are impressive twin staircases, box pews, a mahogany gallery and fine timber coffered ceiling. To its east, towards the river, are the Doric columns of the church school. Almost opposite, Victoria Hall stands on the site of the Victoria Music Hall (built for amateur musicians) where, in 1882, a cornice fell, narrowly missing the novelist Charles Dickens while he was delivering a reading.

Along **Joy Street**, on the right, are the only surviving Georgian city-centre townhouses at ★**Nos. 14–26** ㊷. Once redbrick merchants' homes, they were given over to theatrical lodgings and the street became known as the Street of Ps: Pride, Poverty and Pianos. Nos 36–46 Hamilton Street have similar pasts.

Auctioneers **Ross & Co** occupy the souk-like caverns of Nos 22–26, built in attractive brick and sandstone as the Presbyterian General Assembly's Office in 1875. Veterinary surgeon John Boyd Dunlop, says the plaque, invented the first successful pneumatic tyre at Nos 38–42 and he ran a hospital for sick horses where Telephone House now stands at Nos. 43–71. Facing each other across the Cromac Street/May Street interface are two, now disused, banks designed in the classical manner, both dating from 1919. The Ulster is distinguished by its Baroque cupola.

ST GEORGE'S MARKET

Beyond, on the corner with Verner Street, behind green faïence tiles, stands **Magennis's Whiskey Café**, an attractive bar, sadly known now as the location for the murder of Robert McCartney. The brick, stone and iron **Market House** (1890), sympathetically restored, at a cost of over £4 million, as ★★**St George's Market** ㊸ to the original designs held on linen in City Hall, is all that is left of many such markets that peppered the Laganside end of May Street, in an area still known colloquially as The Markets.

The oldest covered market in Ireland, St George's reopening in 1999 coincided with the movement towards farmers' markets and natural produce, so successfully harnessed at London's Borough Market. With a much smaller base of such suppliers, it has been hard for St George's to rival that level of excellence. However, after a sluggish start, when the large building often seemed half empty on market days, it has really got into its stride. A variety market on Friday (6am–1pm) is a mixture of secondhand and cheap clothes, books, antiques, fruit and veg and 23 fish and seafood stalls.

The **City Food and Garden market** on Saturdays, between 9am and 3pm, has become a genuine draw for foodies with all kinds of (mainly Irish) produce, from the best selection of Irish cheeses in Belfast to a wide range of freshly caught fish and seafood, organic meats and speciality breads as well as various flower stalls.

Voted third best food market in the UK in 2004, St George's also stages various special events and celebrations throughout the year, including craft fairs, Christmas markets and Belfast's main New Year's Eve bash, with more than 3,000 people partying exuberantly in the true Belfast-style.

WATERFRONT HALL

Across the road in what is now Lanyon Place, where noisome, vibrant cattle, flax, fruit, grain, horse, pork, potato, fish and variety markets once thrived, are the spare sandy-coloured towers of the Hilton Hotel, a car park and British Telecom. These almost dwarf the stylishly emblematic ★★★**Belfast Waterfront Hall** ⑭ (2 Lanyon Place, tel: 9033 4455, www.waterfront.co.uk) whose great copper dome is now as much a part of the Belfast skyline as the great shipyard cranes, Samsom and Goliath. Belfast's most prestigious concert venue after the nearby Odyssey Arena, it regularly draws major acts from rock and pop and is also worth checking for drama, ballet, opera and musicals.

Across the street, west through iron security gates at the bottom of Chichester Street, stands the almost white

Star Attractions
● **St George's Market**
● **Waterfront Hall**

Below: statue outside the Waterfront Hall (bottom)

Map on page 20

Below: Queen's Bridge pillar
Bottom: Harmony of Belfast

imposing Portland stone neoclassical bulk of the ★**Royal Courts of Justice** ⓯. Bewigged barristers and pin-striped solicitors parade, clutching pink-ribboned legal bundles while miscreants, plaintiffs and their accusers and pursuers seem (mostly) in awe of the travertine marble vastness of its echoing central hall. Opposite is the Old Town Hall completed in 1870, and now, after much bombing, restored as the **Belfast County Court**.

Downstream towards ★**Queen's Bridge** ⓰ – designed by Charles Lanyon, named after Queen Victoria and built of Newry granite to replace the old Long Bridge which had been *the* place in 1790 for an evening's *paseo,* stands a pedantic cream sandstone perpendicular diversion, once St Malachy's School.

At the corner of Queen's Bridge, at what is now called Thanksgiving Square, visitors can enjoy **Harmony of Belfast**, a recent arrival. Created by Scottish artist Andy Scott, the 19.5-m (64-ft) stainless steel and bronze statue depicts a girl standing on a globe of the world, representing hope, aspiration and spirituality.

ALBERT MEMORIAL CLOCK

Beyond Ann Street along Donegall Quay, past **Tedford's**, a quality bistro that was once a ships' chandlers *(see page 113)* and the **Laganside Bus Centre**, is the city's potentially most appealing vista, ★**Queen's Square** where, until the 1840s, ships tied up at quays named after the Donegall family.

Here stands what once was Ireland's answer to Pisa's leaning tower, topped by the Gothic ★★**Albert Memorial Clock** ⓱. The 34-m (113-ft) column is named after Queen Victoria's stern consort, who is displayed in his Garter robes. Though Lanyon secretly joined the committee that chose its design, a decision to award him the contract was declared improper and the work went to his rival Barre. Built over reclaimed land, where once boats sailed down the River Farset (which now runs underneath), it had developed a serious list to match that of its more illustrious Italian rival. However, a painstaking restoration in 2003 ensured a more solid base and gave it such a thorough cleaning that it looks as new as the day it was built.

★**McHugh's Bar** ⓲, on the left, claims to be Belfast's oldest extant building. Once a raffish collection of bordello taverns (a history reflected in one or two cheeky new details), it included Madame Du Barry's where painter Stanley Spencer supped while his brother

Gilbert 'Professor' Spencer played cathouse piano in the 1940s. Artfully restored by architect Dawson Stelfox, also responsible for the Albert Clock, it's a curious but successful mixture of old and new, with good food and regular music.

Across the square is another of Lanyon's solid accomplishments in Portland stone, rich in Ionic and Doric columns. Built in 1852 for the Northern Bank it is the **First Trust Bank**.

Beyond, to the north, ★**Custom House Square** has recently been restored to become the most important public space in Belfast. What had once been the very lively Belfast version of 'Speakers' Corner' is marked with a life size bronze statue, The Speaker, and includes Belfast's oldest drinking fountain for horses, the Calder fountain, now restored to its former glory. A water feature traces the course of the Farset river beneath and there is a play area for children too.

The purpose of the £4.5 million restoration was to create a public space for special events and, since its launch in 2005, the square has seen everything from strongman competitions, circuses and carnivals to outdoor theatre, festivals and live music of all kinds as well as Belfast's first outdoor Christmas ice rink. It's popular with skateboarders and office workers on sunny days.

CUSTOM HOUSE

The magnificent Palladian simplicity of the ★★★**Custom House** ⑩ itself is the very zenith of Lanyon's achievements. Its real delight is a **pediment** of Britan-

Star Attractions
● **Albert Memorial Clock**
● **Custom House**

Festival time at the Albert Memorial Clock

Map
on page
20

Below: the Custom House
Middle: a popular river cruise
Bottom: aspects of Belfast's
history in the Big Fish's 'skin'

nia, Mercury and Neptune flanked by lion and unicorn, amid capstans and knots, executed by the great stone-mason Thomas Fitzpatrick and seen best from the Lagan Lookout. The novelist Anthony Trollope worked in the Custom House as a post office official in the 1850s.

Now our attention turns to the river. The now defunct Laganside Corporation was set up by the state with a mission to reclaim, revitalise and gentrify the Lagan's banks, an area on which for so long the city had turned its back. First of its conquests had to be the river itself, little more than a mephitic cess of human and industrial effluent, torpid and foul smelling, exposing its detritus-despoiled mudbanks in spring-tide days, dangerous and threatening when its flash-flood storm drains proved less than adequate.

And so a massive purification scheme began. Tributaries were re-culverted, banks dredged and, where previous weirs had ironically served to maximise and retain tidal silting, the new scheme keeps the stream clear, welcoming back plopping grey mullet, the occasional homing Atlantic salmon and increasing numbers of wild brown trout.

THE WATERFRONT

The scheme also maintains a satisfactory water level upstream of **Lagan Weir**. After dusk, blue lighting romanticises the structure. The Belfast and Northern Ireland Welcome Centre has leaflets detailing the 30-plus pieces of imaginative and often quite striking public art dotted around this area, largely created by artists with strong connections to Belfast.

By attracting large levels of investment into the waterfront, the Corporation effectively transformed the area. Large modern apartment blocks overlook the river and a number of new and refurbished buildings now make this one of the prime property locations in Belfast. They have also improved public access, devising, amongst others, an attractive ★★**Riverside Walk** which follows the river upstream from the weir all the way to the Ormeau Bridge and back along the East Bank (you can also try this journey by boat with the Lagan Boat Company, see opposite page).

DONEGALL QUAY

Just downstream of the weir is pedestrianised **Donegall Quay**, with its massive river-wall, bordered on one side with jetties and slipways, on the other by practical but ornamental stone paviours and square-setts pierced by black bollards bearing the gilt seahorse from the city's coat of arms. Near here, in a city which is distinctive for the human scale of its buildings, will be Northern Ireland's tallest building, the 26-storey Obel (standing for 'an obelisk set in old Belfast'), which will include a hotel, luxury apartments and offices.

Here, by the ★★**Big Fish** ⑩ sculpture (a.k.a. the Salmon of Knowledge), which celebrates the return of fish to the Lagan *(see margin note)*, the **Lagan Boat Company** offers very popular *Titanic* boat tours (call the Belfast Welcome Centre for bookings on 9024 6609, or visit www.laganboatcompany.com for more information). On the tours, you can see the drawing rooms where *Titanic* was designed, the dry dock where she was completed, the steam cranes that lowered her down and the slipsteams from which she was launched and get a commentary from genuine enthusiasts. The company also runs a number of special tours, such as Folk on a Boat – as part of the Cathedral Quarter Arts Festival – movie, Christmas and Halloween trips.

THE HARBOUR OFFICE

North along Donegall Quay, past the SeaCat terminal, is **Corporation Square** with its elegant sandstone ★**Harbour Office** ⑪, an Italianate building decked out by Lanyon's partner, W. H. Lynn. Its boardroom, which hosts the captain's table and chairs destined for the *Titanic* but completed too late for the voyage, is rich in fine historical paintings, including one of Captain Pirrie, grandfather to William, whose expansionist vision gave

Star Attractions
● **Riverside Walk**
● **The Big Fish**

The Big Fish
Salmon of Knowledge is a 10-metre (32-ft) ceramic-skinned salmon commissioned to celebrate the return of salmon to the previously polluted River Lagan. Created in 1999 by local artist John Kindness, the sculpture's 'skin' is decorated with a mosaic of texts and messages relating to Belfast's history. Included is material from Tudor times to recent newspaper headlines, along with contributions from Belfast schoolchildren. An 'Ulster Fry' meal, though resolutely non-fishy, is pictured too.

The Big Fish.

Map on page 20

Below: Maritime motifs in the Sinclair Seamen's Church
Bottom: The Odyssey Arena.

birth to the doomed liner. These riches can be inspected on request (tel: 9055 4422).

Just to the west of this is the late-1850s Italianate ★★★**Sinclair Seamen's Presbyterian Church ☻**, designed by Lanyon. Its interior owes more, however, to an optimist and imbiber, the Reverend Sam Cochrane RN. The pitch-pine pulpit has the shape of a ship's prow flanked by navigation lights. The font is a ship's binnacle. The bell of HMS *Hood* calls lost souls to service. Collection boxes take the form of lifeboats. By the door a text reads 'A Merry Heart Doeth Good Like a Medicine'. It is still the traditional duty of each incumbent Minister to visit every ship which docks in Belfast Harbour. The church is open to the public on Wednesday afternoons 2pm–4pm and is well worth a visit.

To the north of the Harbour Office, **Clarendon Road** leads into the newly redeveloped and attractive tree-lined riverside plazas surrounding ★**Clarendon Dock ☻**. The trees are ash and oak, the boulevards laid with stone paviours and square-setts, and many of the laid-up anchors and half-buried cannon bollards authentic.

Barrow Square should be your next target. Its alfresco entertainments include St Patrick's Day traditional music on 17 March and other special live music events. Both nearby pubs, the **Rotterdam** and **Pat's Bar** at the ends, respectively, of Pilot and Prince's Dock Street, which link in with these musical happenings, are highly recommended. The atmospheric Rotterdam has a wide variety of live music to offer, having made a name for itself as the Belfast blues bar. Pat's has concentrated more on traditional Irish music. It was in the Rotterdam

that, allegedly, manacled prisoners were held before deportation to Van Diemen's Land (Tasmania).

Occasionally the evocative portside aromas of grain and flour waft waterwards as they are transported along Corporation Street. Carved symbols in the bright calm of **St Joseph's** Roman Catholic Church, built in 1880 in Prince's Dock Street, echo the maritime theme. Sadly, St Joseph's is now boarded-up and slowly decaying as campaigners battle to save one of the last tangible reminders of life in Sailortown, the name given to this once bustling dockside area, torn apart by motorway development in the 1960s.

Across the Lagan, the huge yellow upturned Us of the cranes, called ★**Samson and Goliath** by all but post-feminists who have rechristened the latter Delilah, dominate the eastern skyline over Queen's Island shipyards. Here Belfast men riveted the great metal skeleton that became the doomed *Titanic* in what were then the world's biggest shipyards.

THE ODYSSEY

Here too, rising above the water is Northern Ireland's landmark Millennium project and its biggest and most multi-faceted visitor attraction, ★★★**the Odyssey** 🟡 (tel: 9045 8806 or visit www.theodyssey.co.uk or www.odysseyarena.com).

The Pavilion offers a variety of ways to keep the kids amused, including the **W5** interactive discovery centre (the five Ws being who, what, where, when and why). With over 140 interactive exhibits, it appeals to children and adults, unaware that scientific principles are being absorbed subliminally as they light lasers, play with walls of sound, walk up musical steps and construct bridges. There's also a 20-lane tenpin bowling alley; Imax cinema with a screen the size of several double-decker buses and 3D capability; 12-screen cinema complex and a number of cafés, bars, restaurants and even nightclubs.

Adjoining, the **Odyssey Arena** is big enough, at 10,000 seats, to attract the top bands and artists in the world, and regularly does *(see also margin note)*.

HIGH STREET

Turning back, through Clarendon Dock and Corporation Street, we turn into Victoria Street and continue until we reach High Street. While the Chapel of the Ford stood on the corner of High Street (left) from at least 1306, its ultimate successor, the high Anglican ★**St George's** 🟡

Star Attractions
● **Sinclair Seamen's Presbyterian Church**
● **The Odyssey**

The Belfast Giants
The Odyssey Arena is regularly transformed into an ice rink for the local Belfast Giants ice hockey team and for various other spectaculars. The Giants are a rather heart-warming success story in that they have built up a non-sectarian supporter base for this exhilarating sport. You can reach the Odyssey by bus from the city-centre or via the bridge by the Lagan Lookout or over Queen Elizabeth Bridge. It also has a large car park.

Goliath

Map on page 20

The Belfast Giants in action at the Odyssey Arena.

Malmaison Hotel

The building is decorated with Thomas Fitzpatrick's splendid stonework, first devised for Lytle's and McCausland's Warehouses, Nos 34–38 Victoria Street. For Lytle he carved frogs between waterlilies, squirrels stuffing with nuts, plus assorted birds and a pig-tailed Chinaman. For McCausland he presented the five trading continents in five robustly non-PC heads: Africa – an Ethiopian slave with broken chain and Nile lily; Asia – a Chinese girl in silks; Oceania – a South Sea Islander with coconuts; Europe – a self-satisfied bewhiskered Caucasian; North America – an indigenous 'Indian' complete with tomahawk and feather head-dress.

dates from only 1813. Its classical portico was brought from the Earl Bishop of Derry's unfinished house. Perks for its first choirboys included all the salmon they could catch from the River Farset beyond the original wrought-iron rear gates. A plain memorial to Henry Pottinger is in tune with its plain interior.

Opposite, on the Bank of Ireland – once the **National Bank –** octagonal fishscale turrets surmount a vigorous facade carved with centaurs and cornucopias.

Just down High Street, at Imperial Buildings, No 72, are the offices of the **Tinderbox Theatre Company**, one of Belfast's most interesting drama companies, with many acclaimed productions to its name at a variety of venues throughout the city.

The **Malmaison Hotel** has a curious frontage *(see panel below and listing on page 126)*. Around the corner, the ever-popular **Milk** nightclub reflects unexpected glamour onto the otherwise well-named Tomb Street.

Bittles' Bar, probably the world's only triangular pub, and packed with literary portraits, is tucked into the grid-iron shaped building at the corner of Victoria Street. The bar was once known as the Shakespeare and was patronised by performers from nearby theatres.

Just across the street, the venerable **Kitchen Bar** has settled in well to its new accommodation, having been forced out of its nearby 1859 premises by the mammoth Victoria Square retail development, which opens in spring 2008.

CHICHESTER STREET

Back, via Montgomery Street, on to Chichester (which locals pronounce *Chai-Chester*) Street, look east for a splendid vista of the Waterfront Hall, then west to the Black Mountain. The pleasant 1810-built **Garrick Bar** at No 29 took its name from the fabled English thespian; its current customers ply other stages, the nearby Petty Sessions and Royal Courts of Justice.

Just west, Nos 7–11 form an excellently restored terrace of four-storey Georgian houses in dusky red brick dating from 1804. They almost complete this route, which now proceeds across Donegall Square East from the red Ballachmoyle sandstone of Ocean Buildings, rich in exotic carvings of mermaids and monsters. For here, right in the corner of the City Hall grounds, there stands – ship's plans at hand – another reminder of *Titanic*: a Sicilian marble ★**statue** of shipbuilder Sir Edward James Harland of Harland & Wolff.

6: North Belfast

Clifton House – Crumlin Road Gaol and Courthouse – The Waterworks – Cave Hill Country Park
– Belfast Castle – McArt's Fort – Cave Hill – Hazelwood – Zoo

Star Attraction
● Clifton House

Once known as the Poorhouse, ★★★**Clifton House** ⑤⑥ at
Carlisle Circus, though much altered, is still one of the
most delightfully modest public Georgian buildings in
Ireland and one of Belfast's oldest. A central two-storey
redbrick block is flanked by single-storey wings with
gabled end pavilions and its octagonal central tower
forms a pleasing focal point. In still spacious grounds
donated by Lord Donegall, it was opened in 1774 by the
Belfast Charitable Society to house the poor and indi-
gent, hosting grand balls to pay for their upkeep. Today,
after a lengthy restoration, the building is shared by a
sheltered housing association and a new interpretative
centre (visits by prior arrangement, tel: 9033 4215).

Below: Clifton House
*Bottom: Belfast seen
from Cave Hill*

For those interested in the United Irishmen, it's an
important port of call. Robert Joy and his co-editor
brother, Henry, were uncles to rebel leader Henry Joy
McCracken, hanged in 1798, after which the military,
housed next door, gave them 48 hours to clear the Poorhouse. Henry Joy McCracken's sister, the early feminist
Mary Ann, who tried vainly to save her brother and was
to bring up his illegitimate child, became a tireless cam-
paigner for social justice throughout her long life,
devoting herself to the welfare of the Poorhouse residents and many other social and political causes.

Map
on page
66

The Great Rebellion

Henry Joy McCracken, who lies in Clifton Street burial ground, was one of the founders in 1791 of the Society of United Irishmen. He was a Presbyterian cotton manufacturer and is a reminder that not all the opposition to English rule in Ireland came from oppressed Roman Catholics. Along with Wolfe Tone, also a Protestant, he organised an armed rebellion in 1798. But the 'Great Rebellion' was ruthlessly put down and McCracken was executed.

Virtually opposite is the ★**Indian Community Centre**, at 86 Clifton Street, housing a Hindu temple. The ICC hosts many social events throughout the year, including the Mela festival in August, which brings thousands to Botanic Park for Indian dancing, music, fashion and food. Increasingly pro-active, it co-organises a Diwali/Celtic festival of light each October.

Lanyon aficionados will soldier on north up Clifton Street, under the unbending gaze of Harry Hems' striking 3-m (10-ft) 3-ton life-sized bronze of ★**King Billy**, sabre drawn, the city's sole equestrian monument on the roof of **Clifton Street Orange Hall**.

One of the most important burial sites in Belfast is the Clifton Street burial ground, where many pioneers of Belfast life lie, including politicians, journalists, Henry Joy McCracken (*see margin note*) and his sister Mary Ann, and the man who coined the phrase 'Emerald Isle', Dr William Drennan. There are graveyard tours at various times of the year, such as Hallowe'en.

THE OLD GAOL

North past Carlisle Circus are Lanyon's deliberately sinister Piranesian ★★**Crumlin Road Gaol** ❺⑦ and his formidable Corinthian ★**Crown Courthouse,** facing each other across, and joined by a tunnel below, the Crumlin Road.

The atmospheric Gaol, which closed in 1966, has been the venue for theatrical events and other attractions since. One of Belfast's most important Victorian buildings, it is to undergo a major £1 million restoration programme, which will include its facade being restored to its original glory. The Courthouse is scheduled to be converted to luxury flats.

A further Lanyon delight, **St Paul's** Church of Ireland, improves the view from the unlovely Yorkgate train station on York Street. Further up, at 333 Crumlin Road, in a beautiful converted mill, is the ★**Flax International Arts Centre's** Golden Thread Dance Studio and Theatre ❺⑧ (tel: 9074 5421) and the independent Golden Thread Gallery (tel: 9035 2333).

Returning to Carlisle Circus, turn into the lengthy **Antrim Road**, and you'll find the pleasant **Waterworks Park**, dating from an 1840s attempt to solve Belfast's growing water needs.

Looking west, north or east from almost any-

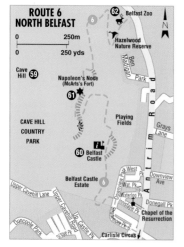

ROUTE 6 NORTH BELFAST

0   250m
0   250 yds

Belfast Zoo ❻②

Hazelwood Nature Reserve

Cave Hill ❺⑨

Napoleon's Nose (McArts's Fort) ❻①

CAVE HILL COUNTRY PARK

Playing Fields

Grays Lane

❻⓪ Belfast Castle

Belfast Castle Estate

Upper Cavehill Lane
Upper Cavehill Road

West Pk
Wat. Pk
Downview Ave
Waterloo Pk
Donegall Pk

Chapel of the Resurrection

Carlisle Circus

where in Belfast you can see that the city is cupped in a saucer of hills. Clockwise from the west, they are the **Black Mountain**, **Cave Hill**, the **Castlereagh Hills** and the drumlins of County Down, all framed at the ends of the shallow canyons of the streets.

Most spectacular is the profile of ★★**Cave Hill 59**, 'Napoleon's Nose' to locals. One of the finest views of Belfast can be obtained after the 6-km (4-mile) climb up the hill to look down on the Lagan estuary with the sprawl of Belfast for miles below. The hill has eight waymarked trails, popular with walkers and joggers. Environmental campaigners have opposed a recent cable car scheme and plans for a hotel on the hill.

Any Metro bus with a 1 (A–F) will take you from Antrim Road to Belfast Zoo, with a stop at suburban **Strathmore Park** from where the climb begins, first past the castle's isolated turreted former **gatelodge**, designed by Charles Lanyon's son, John. Then uphill and right along **Downview Park West** with the castle's Gothic former **mortuary chapel** to the right in Innisfayle Park.

BELFAST CASTLE

A left turn brings us into **Belfast Castle Estate** and up to the ★★**Castle 60** (tel: 9077 6925) a ruggedly romantic Scots baronial pile rich in turrets and faced with Cookstown sandstone. It was constructed in 1865 for the impoverished 3rd marquis of Donegall, again by John Lanyon, who borrowed freely from Prince Albert's sketches for his recently completed Balmoral Castle. Lanyon Jr's fees were guaranteed by the marquis's

Star Attractions
● Crumlin Road Gaol
● Cave Hill
● Belfast Castle

Below: a guide takes tourists round a Crumlin Road estate
Bottom: Belfast Castle

Map
on page
66

Star Attraction
● Belfast Zoo

Residents of Belfast Zoo

daughter, Harriet, who had taken the precaution of marrying the immensely rich 8th earl of Shaftesbury. Their son, the 9th earl, presented the castle to the city in 1934.

Walkers should call in at the useful **Visitor Centre** at the Castle for detailed maps and a history and overview of the area. Tours of the Castle are available and there is a restaurant, bar and antiques shop in the cellar. There's an excellent adventure playground in the grounds for three to 14-year-olds (open seven days Apr–Sept, weekends only Oct–Mar).

NAPOLEON'S NOSE

However, the Cave Hill walk proper through the 200-acre estate begins in the car park a bit further downhill, climbing on gravelled paths up to a T-junction where the correct direction is right, giving a view of the castle below as you continue through the woods, taking main turns left, then upward.

Out from the woods a steeper path takes a left right up to the mouth of the titular **cave** first used by Neolithic hunter-gatherers. Just before the cave-mouth, a further left runs even more steeply towards what looks like a notch in the skyline but which is in fact a defensive ditch to **McArt's Fort** on the 400-m (1,180-ft) high promontory. This is alternatively referred to as ★**Napoleon's Nose ❺** or **Ben Madigan** (from *beann*, the Irish for peak) after a 9th-century King of Ulster.

Foxes trail rabbits through heather. Kestrel and peregrine hover and stoop. Badgers wander at night through the Maytime bluebells. Yet, below, Belfast sprawls.

BELFAST ZOO

The route continues due north towards (but not too near) the cliff's edge, before descending alongside a stream through **Hazelwood Nature Reserve**. This brings you on to a better path, then steps, to the perimeter of the ★★**Zoo ❻**, whose entrance is to the left (hours from opening to last admissions – closing times are two hours later – are: Apr–Sept, 10am–5pm; Oct–Mar, 10am–2.30pm).

Built in the early 19th century as part of a pleasure ground at the end of the tram route, the zoo has a pleasantly old-fashioned feel, but, in fact, is considered remarkably progressive in its captive breeding programme for rare animals. Lemurs are allowed to stroll freely around the zoo. The African Enclosure and the penguin and sea lion pools are popular with children.

7: West Belfast

Shankill Road – Peace Wall – Lower Falls – Falls Road – Political Tours – An Cultúrlann – City and Milltown Cemeteries – Casement Park – Black Mountain

If you're looking for the famous political wall murals, from King Billy to hunger-striker Bobby Sands, memorial plots, peace walls and many of the most famous landmarks from over three decades of globally reported violence, west Belfast is the place to start. For those who assume the area is solely republican, one of the most striking features they will find is just how closely situated are the two most iconic roads belonging to the two communities, the Shankill and Falls.

TOURS OF THE TROUBLES

Over the years a thriving industry has developed around the legacy of the Troubles, resulting in a pretty comprehensive choice of tours in the area. Several bus and coach tours take in the main sites of west Belfast, either specifically or as part of citywide tours, and you will also discover a wide range of Black Taxi tours for a more personalised touch.

However, the most authentic and detailed tours are those organised by republican and loyalist former prisoners. The republican ex-prisoners' group **Coiste** (10 Beechmount Avenue, tel: 9020 0770 or visit www.coiste.ie/politicaltours) run daily political tours, meeting at Divis Tower in the Lower Falls at 11am and

> **The "Peace Line"**
> On 9 September 1969, James Chichester-Clarke, prime minister of Northern Ireland's parliament, announced that the British army would build a temporary "peace line" between Protestant and Catholic areas of Belfast to stop rioting. By the end of the century there were 15 walls separating the two communities, some corrugated-iron barriers crowned with razor wire, others 6-metre (20-ft) concrete barricades reminiscent of the Berlin Wall. The most obtrusive stretched for 3km (2 miles), separating the Falls and Shankill Roads. The walls have now become a tourist attraction, but some locals believe they are still needed.

Black taxis provide transport for locals and tourists

A traditional Ulster Fry, not approved by cardiologists

visiting sites of historic and political significance on the Falls Road. These are walking tours and can last up to three hours. Tickets can be bought at the Belfast Welcome Centre (tel: 9024 6609) and booking is essential. If you are part of a large group and can give a few days' notice,

Coiste can also custom-make tours, organising meetings with victim's and lobby groups and even politicians. In a sign of the changing times, they will even organise a joint tour with ex-loyalist prisoners, handing your group over at the peace wall. These prearranged tours can be expensive, so the larger the group the less impact on your wallet.

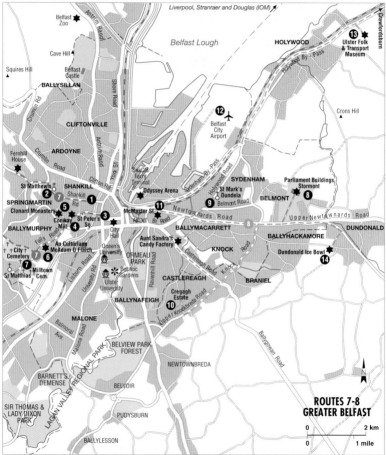

ROUTES 7-8
GREATER BELFAST

SHANKILL ROAD

For those who prefer to make their own way, the **Shankill Road ❶**, at the bottom of west Belfast is probably the best place to start. Although the presence of loyalist paramilitaries is still keenly felt, the introduction of the £4.5 million **Shankill Centre** (331–333 Shankill Road, tel: 9050 4555) in 2001, a rough equivalent of **An Cultúrlann McAdam Ó Fiaich** on the Falls, has become a base for local community groups as well as dance, drama and music studios, sports venues, a film society and a café with a good Ulster Fry on the menu.

To take in most of what the road has to offer by foot, begin at the base and move up, stopping first at the 1896 **Shankill Road Mission**, whose founder, the Rev Henry Montgomery, theatrically signed the famous Covenant objecting to the Home Rule Bill of 1912 in his own blood. You could also take a short detour left here to Northumberland Avenue which takes you up the peace wall where it meets the Falls Road.

Back on the Shankill Road, past the **Rex Bar** and the famous mural of Edward Carson signing the 1912 Covenant, and you will come to the **Shankill Memorial Gardens**, on the other side of the road, which recalls those who died in the two world wars, with a street lamp with an 'eternal' flame recalling a Shankill Road bombing in 1993.

Towards the top of the road, on the right, is the **Shankill Graveyard**, the main city cemetery until 1866. It contains the graves of several notable citizens as well as many who died in the various plagues. The name Shankill comes from the Gaelic for 'Old Church', the site of which, believed to date from the 6th century, can be found within the graveyard.

Just up the road, you'll find the distinctive 1872 Church of Ireland **★★St Matthew's ❷**, known as the 'Shamrock Church', for its tri-cornered shape, whose holy water font is believed to be the only remnant in Belfast of the original Old Church (and is also believed to be a cure for warts!). Nearby is another famous mural, depicting James Buchanan, one of several US presidents with Ulster antecedents.

THE PEOPLE'S CABS

One of the best ways to see west Belfast is by shared black cab. Almost as famous around the world as those of London (where many of them began life) they origi-

Star Attractions
● St Matthew's Church
● Fernhill House

The Falls and Shankill
Though lack of resources and poverty still affect both communities, they seem much more pronounced in the Shankill, a heartland of loyalism. Redevelopment has not been sympathetic or universal, with many empty sites and decaying buildings, and it is estimated that nearly half the population of the area has departed over the past two and a half decades. Compared to the more cohesive and vibrant republican community on the Falls, there is a noticeable listlessness and lack of bustle. This is typified by the areas' two summer festivals, with the nationalist West Belfast Festival (Féile an Phobail), claiming to be Europe's biggest community-led festival, dwarfing the far more modest Shankill version.

Old-style shopping on the Shankill Road

Map on page 70

Below: Clonard Monastery
Bottom: a mural remembers
Bobby Sands, who starved
to death in jail in 1981

nated during the Troubles when the burning of buses meant locals had to find alternative means of transport. The West Belfast Taxi Association (tel: 028 9031 5777. www.wbta.net) operates taxis up and down the Falls Road, with adult fares of just over £1 for most routes.

But if you want to see the best of the Shankill for a similar outlay try the shared cab service run by the North Belfast Mutual Association (400 Shankill Road, tel: 028 9032 8775). Leaving from North Street and Bridge Street, their cabs will take you down the Shankill Road for just 80p.

It's a great way to get chatting to local people, who, despite the reputation of the area, are invariably friendly and talkative. For a little more, NBMA cabs will take you to Glencairn, Springmartin and Silverstream (leaving from North Street) and Monkstown, Rathcoole and even to the coastal town of Carrickfergus (leaving from Bridge Street).

At the apex of nearby Woodvale and **Crumlin Road,** the peaceline marks off Catholic Ardoyne, beside where 20,000 were employed in the once-great linen mills. In recent times, the area has been known as a regular flashpoint during the summer's marching season and the location of the infamous Holy Cross school protests.

FALLS ROAD

For republican west Belfast, it's easier to begin the tour anew, down near the city-centre, at the lower end of the Falls Road ❸. Though many high-rise, low-income tower blocks have been demolished, the area still displays many icons illustrating passions that tore the area

apart. Divis Tower is still called *Planet of the IRSPs* (Irish Republican Socialist Party). On **St Peter's Square**, off the Falls Road, the eponymous pro-Cathedral's twin spires lined up the sights of World War II German bombers. At Sevastapol Street, and thence uphill, the memorial murals are for Bobby Sands, elected MP as he lay dying, who was the first of the 10 republican hunger-strikers to die, after a 66-day fast in 1981.

The first stop should be ★**Conway Mill** ❹ at 5–7 Conway Street (tel: 9024 9323). Built in 1842 by the Kennedy family, it was the first flax spinning mill in west Belfast and though many would follow, it is now the last remaining in the area.

Linen was the industry Belfast was built on and west Belfast owes much of its sudden (mostly Catholic) population growth at the time to the industry. The Mill, now a listed building, ceased production in 1972 and is now a centre for local businesses. 22 artists and crafts-people (wood carving and turning, ceramics, jewellery, glassware, paintings and furniture etc) also work and exhibit there. A shop sells their work and that of others. There's also an exhibition on the history of linen, and a theatre. Guided tours of the mill can be arranged.

Star Attraction
● **Clonard Monastery & Church**

> **Linen's heyday**
> In this area, only Flax and Cambrai Streets remind us of the linen mills' raw material, flax grown from seed imported from the Belgian town of Cambrai. Until the 1930s schoolkids followed four hours in the mills with four tired hours in school, trapping themselves, ill educated, into a short, unhealthy linen lifetime while the rich carelessly spilled claret on the hard-wrought damask.

CLONARD MONASTERY

A little further up the Falls Road, at the end of Clonard Street, is the impressive ★★**Clonard Monastery and Church** ❺ (tel: 9044 5950). Built in French Gothic-style with a striking 6m-wide (20-ft) stained-glass rose window, the church and monastery were completed in 1911. You can trace the history of its owners, the Redemptorist order, a Catholic movement founded in Italy in 1732, on floor and ceiling mosaics as you enjoy the Portland stone and marble columns of its interior. Usually in early summer, the Church hosts a nine-day Novena when the grounds are crowded with the faith-ful. It is here that vital talks were held that ultimately led to the peace process. The church is also used as part of the West Belfast Festival.

On the other side of the Falls Road, **Dunville Park** is named after its whiskey-distilling benefactor, who donated the park to the people of the city in 1887. Located within the park is the famous Dunville Foun-tain. Further up the road, the sprawling grounds of Roy-al Victoria Hospital still house the world's first air con-ditioning ducts. Near here is the high-quality hostel, **Farset International** *(see page 127)*. Another regular

Relaxing in the park

Below: Falls Road retailing
Bottom: street parade during
the West Belfast Festival

venue for the West Belfast Festival (as part of their International Day) is **St Mary's University College**. Designed in the High Victorian style and dating from 1900, it is part of Queen's University. Manchester United fans will find a home from home at the **Red Devils** pub across the road.

★★An Cultúrlann McAdam Ó Fiaich ❻ ((216 Falls Road, tel: 9096 4188) is a three-storey Irish language, arts and cultural centre that has operated out of a former Presbyterian Church since 1991. It has a restaurant, Irish language book and gift shop (with an excellent selection of Irish traditional music CDs), theatre, exhibition space and tourist information point. Two traditional music sessions are held during the week.

The **West Belfast (Féile An Phobail) Festival** office, open most of the year as it has a children's festival in March to organise too, is just up the road at Teach na Féile (No. 473, tel: 9031 3440). Usually held in early August, the festival is a mixture of all kinds of music, drama, literary events and comedy, with major names like Roddy Doyle, Christy Moore and Stephen Rea, mixing with local street sports and republican exhibitions. Highlights include the heated political debates and a colourful parade up the Falls.

CEMETERY STORIES

Though it might seem perverse, one of the most fascinating tours in Belfast is during the festival when a local Sinn Féin councillor, Tom Hartley, takes visitors on a daily 90-minute journey around the **★★City Cemetery ❼ and Milltown Cemetery**, the former owned by Belfast City Council and the latter by the Catholic

Church. Milltown, where, on live TV, loyalist paramilitary Michael Stone shot and threw grenades at mourners at a republican funeral, includes the plot where hunger striker Bobby Sands and others are buried.

Despite the sunken wall that prevents Catholic and Protestant bodies from mingling underground, the real story of the City Cemetery is more complex. Here lie the Great and Good of Belfast, men who shaped the city. Yet, the most striking features of their tombs are the Celtic Crosses and the seeming acceptance of a cultural Irishness that would have contrasted sharply with their political loyalties. Reach 1921, and the effects of partition become apparent in an absence of Irish symbols and the frequency of Union Jacks. Both cemeteries can be visited within normal opening hours.

Roughly between Milltown cemetery and motorway is the unlikely location for the 53-acre **Bog Meadows nature reserve** (free entry), a haven for birdwatchers.

Wander off the Falls Road and names of the housing estates will be familiar from the news accounts of the Troubles: **Springmartin, Ballymurphy, New Barnsley and Andersonstown**.

If you turn right at the City Cemetery, and climb the hill you'll find another of these well-known estates, **Whiterock** – where the British Army took their barracks underground. Here, at the **Theatre On the Rock**, is the current home of DubbelJoint (Dub for Dublin/Bel for Belfast) Theatre Company, which has produced some of the finest and most challenging theatre to come out of Ireland. Here it was that Marie Jones's *Stones in his Pocket* first premiered – for years, Jones was a leading actor and writer for the company.

CASEMENT PARK

Further on is Falls Park and, near the now-deserted Andersonstown Police Barracks, the **Felon's Club**, whose membership is restricted to ex-republican prisoners (visitors are welcome, particularly at festival time). Close by is **Casement Park**, Belfast home of the Gaelic Athletic Association sports of hurling and football.

Further afield is the distinctive **St Matthias Church**, off the Glen Road, which belonged to the Church of Ireland and is known as the 'Tin Church'.

Even further out is the beautiful **★Divis and Black Mountain**, opened by the National Trust in 2005, with delightful walks and great views over the city and, on a clear day, across to Scotland and the Isle of Man.

Star Attractions
● **An Cultúrlann McAdam Ó Fiaich**
● **City Cemetery**

Last Resting Place
In the City Cemetery lie Lord Pirrie, Chairman of Harland and Wolff when *Titanic* was built, and later to become, to the surprise of all, a Home Ruler. Here too is Robert Lynd, a republican socialist of Presbyterian stock, who wrote the introduction to James Connelly's *Labour and Irish History*, and Vere Foster, whose copy book was used throughout the British Empire to teach children the art of copperplate writing.

Gaelic football at Casement Park

Map on page 70

Neglecting Lewis
Belfast has been slow to catch on to the potential worth of its more famous citizens, and C. S. Lewis is no exception. Though he wrote fondly of his boyhood years in east Belfast and often yearned for the familiar sounds of the ships' hooters in nearby Belfast Lough, his first home, in Dundela, no longer exists (though a blue plaque marks the spot) and the council missed an opportunity to buy its successor. However, the council has to some extent redeemed itself with the inception of a popular C.S. Lewis Festival each December, celebrating the author's links with the area.

Below: C.S. Lewis's The Lion, the Witch and the Wardrobe *was given the Disney movie treatment in 2005*

8: East Belfast

Stormont – C. S. Lewis, George Best and Van Morrison – Templemore Avenue – Belfast City Airport – Holywood – Old Inn – Ulster Folk and Transport Museum – Culloden Hotel – Dundonald Ice Bowl

A huge, disparate section of the city, with many suburbs, parks and estates, east Belfast is too formless, too rambling, to divide into routes. Furthermore, we have already dealt with its greatest current and future attractions (the Odyssey and shipyards) in the Titanic Quarter. But there is still much to see here, from Stormont Castle to the origins of an unlikely trio of local famous sons, C. S. Lewis, Van Morrison and George Best.

STORMONT

In some ways, one could argue that the most influential building in Belfast is the ★★**Parliament Buildings**, **Stormont** ❽, off the Upper Newtownards Road. Its endless driveway leads through extensive parkland to the Scottish baronial-style Stormont Castle, bought by the new Northern Ireland government in the early 1920s and opened as the Parliament Building in 1932. Over the past few years, it has operated only intermittently as the seat of government for Northern Ireland, depending on the current health of the peace process. **Belfast City Sightseeing** runs a Stormont bus tour from the City centre, which also stops at the Harland and Wolff shipyard.

COP SHOP

Those with a benign interest in police uniforms and firearms can visit the **Police Museum** at Police HQ by appointment (65 Knock Road, tel: 9065 0222 ext 22499; Mon–Fri; free). Exhibits go back as far as 1822.

C. S. LEWIS

With the 2005 release of the film of *The Chronicles of Narnia: The Lion, the Witch and the Wardrobe*, **C. S. Lewis** (1898–1963), the author of the acclaimed children's books and a noted writer on Christianity, achieved a much higher profile in his native city. The best tour is run by Lewis enthusiast Ken Harper (tel: 9074 2711 or visit www.harperstaxitours.co.nr) who will take you to inspect the Linen Hall Library's C. S. Lewis collection, **St Mark's Dundela** ❾, the church where Jack (the name Lewis preferred to Clive) saw his fearsome grandfather preach each Sunday, the house he grew up in at Little Lea (and in whose attic flourished the youthful imagination and creativity that led to Narnia) and the wardrobe sculpture at nearby Holywood Arches dedicated to him. *(See also pages 110–111).*

Ken Harper also arranges tours to explore the origins of the late George Best (including the house in the **Cregagh Estate ⑩** where the celebrated footballer grew up and where his father still lives) and Van Morrison, who sang about his childhood home on **Hyndford Street** (a blue plaque adorns No 125), as he did about the nearby and much grander Cyprus Avenue and several other local locations. Morrison fanatics may want to stay at **Bowden's B&B** *(see page 127),* just off Cyprus Avenue and run by fellow devotee Carole Bowden.

You can still get a glimpse of East Belfast's prosperous industrial era around the **Newtownards Road/ Templemore Avenue** junction, near which the old working-class housing has been preserved at ★**McMaster Street ⑪**. Around the corner are the old Templemore Baths. Opposite **St Matthew's Catholic Church** is the Protestant, **St Patrick's** – the 'Shipyard Church'. The junction also has numerous murals close to loyalist hearts. The celebrated flautist James Galway once played in a local flute band.

WHERE CANDY IS DANDY

Nearby, at 60 Castlereagh Road, history of a more pleasant kind can be found at **Aunt Sandra's Candy Factory** (tel: 9073 2868; Mon–Fri 9.30am–4.30pm, Sat 9.30am–5pm; free), where children can watch sweets and chocolates being made in traditional ways.

Star Attraction
● **Parliament Buildings**

Below: Aunt Sandra's Candy Factory
Bottom: Stormont, built for Northern Ireland's parliament

Map on page 70

Star Attractions
● Old Inn, Crawfordsburn
● Ulster Folk and Transport Museum

Holywood

Belfast's George Best Airport ⑫, a couple of miles up from the Titanic Quarter, is just a few minutes' drive from the heart of the city. Just further on from here, the attractive, residential town of **Holywood** has some excellent restaurants and cafés. A church existed here as early as the 7th century. Though only a 15-minute drive from the city centre, along the Lough, it is already beginning to feel like the country.

Within the next few miles are delightful walks in beautiful Loughside reserves like Helen's Bay and the atmospheric ★★**Old Inn** *(listing, page 127)* at pretty **Crawfordsburn**, beloved by C. S. Lewis, who stayed there on his bittersweet honeymoon with his dying wife, Joy.

Ulster Folk and Transport Museum

The Ulster Folk and Transport Museum at Cultra

Even closer to Holywood is one of Ireland's most popular tourist attractions, the excellent ★★★**Ulster Folk and Transport Museum** ⑬ (tel: 9042 8428, www.uftm.org.uk, admission fee, open daily) at Cultra *(see page 120)*. Farm-houses, cottages, churches and mills have been painstakingly reconstructed – often brick by brick from their original locations. One of Belfast's three five-star hotels, the **Culloden** *(listing, page 126)*, is also here.

Finally, those with children to entertain will find a trio of usefully adjacent family attractions in the otherwise un-touristy Dundonald area. The two **Pirates Adventure Golf** courses, replete with pirate schooner, are next door to the Olympic-sized ice rink and state-of-the-art bowling alley at the **Dundonald Ice Bowl** ⑭, while all kinds of domesticated animals await at the **Streamvale Open Farm** *(see page 120)*.

9. Riverside Walks

Map on page 70

For those who want a pleasant walk near the heart of the city, follow the circular **Riverside Walkway** upstream to Ormeau Bridge. Starting at **Lagan Weir** the walkway heads south past Queen's Bridge and along the left bank skirting Waterfront Hall, the Hilton and the BT building to the Edge pub at May's Meadow.

Below: on the Lagan Towpath
Bottom: Sir Thomas and
Lady Dixon Park

From there it crosses East Bridge Street to St George's Harbour and continues past the Gasworks regeneration and Haulier's Walk to Ormeau Bridge.

ORMEAU PARK

It continues across the bridge and downstream along the **Ormeau Embankment** (with pleasant Ormeau Park on the right) to Ravenhill Reach, losing the river along Ravenhill Road, but rejoining it at Pottinger's Quay. Then come Laganview and Gregg's Quay, and to the north of the Queen's Bridge **Abercorn Basin**, whose attractions include the Odyssey Pavilion and Arena.

It is also possible to explore the wooded parkland off the **Lagan Towpath** further upstream. Here, linen barons' mansions recall the Lagan Canal's part in a grandiose 19th-century scheme to create an inland Belfast to Dublin water route. Walks begin on Lockview Road, alfresco, at **Cutter's Wharf**'s Bar and Grill.

LAGAN VALLEY NATURE RESERVE

The path descends through wildflower grasslands, into the Ulster Wildlife Trust's **Lagan Valley Nature Reserve** and across the Lagan Canal. Another footbridge, across the River Lagan, leads into **Belvoir Forest Park**. Otherwise follow the left bank of the Lagan downstream, crossing a wooded island between canal and river. A footbridge crosses the canal, leading back to Cutter's Wharf.

BARNETT'S DEMESNE

Left-bank explorers can continue upstream by **Clement Wilson Park**, and past the 1709 **Shaw's Bridge**. From here there's a possible diversion to **Barnett's Demense** with its elegant 1820s house, restaurant and art gallery.

Another 10 km (6 miles) takes in **Sir Thomas and Lady Dixon Park** with its mansion and magnificent rolling acres. Following the right bank upstream a 6-km (4-mile) loop takes you past the linen village of **Edenderry** to the **Giant's Ring** dolmen and back by road.

Further Information
Belfast City Parks (tel: 028 9032 0202 or visit www.parks.belfastcity.gov.uk) publishes a useful booklet, *A Walk in the Park.* For bus and train information, contact Translink (tel: 028 9066 6630 or visit www.translink.co.uk).

EXCURSIONS FROM BELFAST

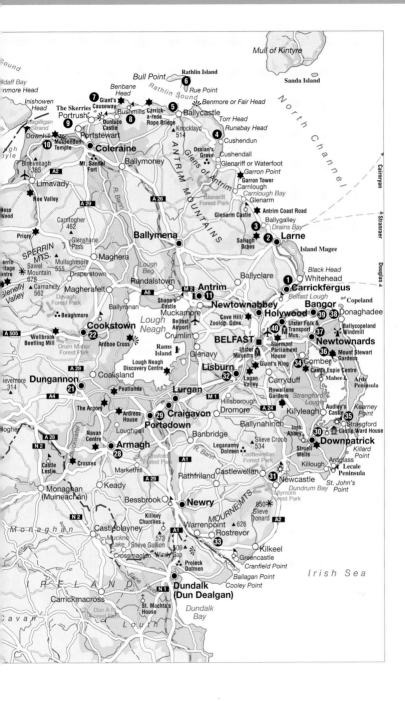

The Antrim Coast Road and on to the Giant's Causeway

Carrickfergus – Larne – Ballygalley – Cushendun – Cushendall – Ballycastle – Rathlin – Giant's Causeway – Bushmills – Portrush – Portstewart – Downhill

Star Attraction
● Carrickfergus

A good ring-road system takes you through the city to the north shore of Belfast Lough, through the well-to-do suburbs of **Whiteabbey** and **Greenisland**, and on to **★★Carrickfergus ❶**, a market town 19 km (12 miles) north from Belfast along the A2. Its big synthetic-fibre plants have gone, but an imposing 13th-century Norman **Castle** (Marine Highway, tel: 9335 1273, admission fee, closed Sunday am) recalls gun-running exploits early in the 20th century. It is a real castle in every sense, with a portcullis, ramparts looking out over the sea, chilling dungeons, cannons and a regimental museum in the keep. Looking to the new age of leisure, the town's **marina** has 300 berths. The parish church of St Nicholas (with stained-glass windows to Santa Claus) is 12th-century.

In Antrim Street, **Carrickfergus Museum** (tel: 9335 8049, free, open seven days a week) outlines the town's history. **Flame!** (44 Irish Quarter West, tel: 9336 9575, admission fee, Jul–Aug 10am–6pm daily, Apr–Jun, Sept 2–6pm) is Ireland's only gasworks museum; you can climb the gasholder for panoramic views. A mile to the east, the **Andrew Jackson Cottage** (Boneybefore, tel: 9335 8049, free, open Apr–Oct, call for precise times) is a re-construction of the ancestral thatched cottage of Andrew Jackson, seventh President of the United States.

UNSPOILT BEACHES

The countryside north of Carrickfergus becomes rich meadow land, with the sleepy seaside town of **Whitehead,** base for the Railway Preservation Society of Ireland (Castleview Road, Whitehead, tel: 2826 0803, occasional steam excursions). The town nestles at the mouth of the lough, with a seashore walk to the Black Head lighthouse. Beyond this begins the peninsula of **Island Magee**, with unspoilt beaches and caves, which wraps around Larne Lough. From here, the road runs into unlovely **Larne ❷**, a port with frequent ferries to and from Stranraer in Scotland (70 minutes away). The Larne and District Historical Centre at 2 Victoria Road (tel: 2827 9482, free, opening hours vary) has a historical centre featuring photographs from 100 years ago.

Crises in Carrickfergus

Carrickfergus, celebrated in a song sung by Van Morrison, has good stories to tell. Its castle was besieged for a year in 1315 by Edward Bruce's Scottish invaders. William of Orange first set foot on Irish soil here on his way to defeat James II at the Battle of the Boyne in 1690 and thus secure the English throne for Protestantism. The French, intermittent allies of Irish nationalists, briefly captured the town in 1760. The port was used for gun-running in 1912–14 as Unionist militants armed themselves to resist Britain's granting Home Rule to Ireland.

Left: Carrickfergus Castle
Below: the town's marina

Map
on pages
80–81

Antrim's glens

At various points, you can turn into one or other of Antrim's celebrated nine glens – Glenarm, Glencloy, Glenariff, Glenballyeamon, Glenaan, Glencorp, Glendun, Glenshesk and Glentaisie – and into another world. It's a world of weather-beaten farmers in tweeds and baggy trousers; a world of sheep sales conducted by auctioneers who talk like machine guns; a world with a baffling dialect that turns an ewe into a yow and "six" into sex; a world where poteen, illicit (and potentially lethal) alcohol, is distilled in lonely places.

Jollity during the Auld Lammas Fair in Ballycastle

THE ANTRIM COAST ROAD

The rewards of continuing along the coast are spectacular views of brown moorlands, white limestone, black basalt, red sandstone and blue sea along the ★★★**Antrim Coast Road**. A notable engineering achievement, it is explained in the Larne Interpretive Centre (Narrow Gauge Road, tel: 2826 0088, free; Oct–Easter Mon–Fri; Easter–Sept Mon–Sat). The road, designed in 1834 by Sir Charles Lanyon as a work of famine relief, opened up an area whose inhabitants had previously found it easier to travel by sea to Scotland than overland to the rest of Ireland.

Ballygalley ❸, at the start of the famous scenic drive, has a 1625 fortified manor house (now a hotel) and, inland from the coast road, a well-preserved old mill and pottery. **White Bay** is a picnic area around which small fossils can be found. **Glenarm** has a beautiful park adjoining a fussy castle, home of the Earls of Antrim. **Carnlough** has a fine harbour and, running over its main street, a white bridge built in 1854 to carry limestone from the quarries to waiting boats. The Londonderry Arms hotel (also 1854) retains the charms of an old coaching inn.

An Irish song-and-dance festival is held each July in the village of **Waterfoot**. This is also the entrance to **Glenariff Glen**, a deep wooded gorge dubbed by Thackeray "Switzerland in miniature". Wild flowers carpet the upper glen in spring and early summer, and slippery rustic footbridges carry walkers over the Glenariff River, past postcard-pretty waterfalls.

About 2 km (1½ miles) to the north, **Cushendall**, "capital of the glens", was created largely by a wealthy 19th-century landowner, Francis Turnly. His most striking structure was the four-storey red sandstone **Curfew Tower**, built as "a place of confinement for idlers and rioters". The village has a good beach and is a popular sailing centre. Just to the north is **Layde Old Church**, dating back to the 13th century and containing some ancient vaults. Ten km (6 miles) further on, ★**Cushendun ❹** is a village of charming Cornish-style white cottages, graceful old houses and friendly pubs, has been captured on countless canvases and the entire place is protected by the National Trust.

THE NORTHERN COAST

Crossing the towering **Glendun Viaduct** (1839), one passes the ruins of **Bonamargy Friary**, founded around 1500. A vault contains the massive coffins of several

MacDonnell chieftains who stood out successfully against the forces of England's Queen Elizabeth I. Nearby, **Corrymeela Community House** is an inter-denominational conference and holiday centre, whose idealism shines out amid Northern Ireland's prevailing political cynicism.

Star Attraction
● **Antrim Coast Road**

The best time to visit ★**Ballycastle** ❺ is during the **Auld Lammas Fair**, held on the last Monday and Tuesday of August. Then this unspoiled town turns into one throbbing market place as farmers with impenetrable accents bring their livestock in from the glens and hundreds of stalls sell souvenirs, bric-a-brac, dulse (dried, edible seaweed) and yellowman (a sweet confectionery). The big attraction is the *craic* – pronounced "crack" (a Scots-Irish word for talk, enlivened by a glass or two of Bushmills). It's great fun – an authentic folk event that owes nothing to the manipulations of tourist boards. The **Ballycastle Museum** (59 Castle Street, tel: 2076 2024, free, open July–Aug) concentrates on the folk social history of the Glens.

Below: climbers at Fair Head, east of Ballycastle
Bottom: Cushendun

A sea-front memorial marks the spot where, in 1898, Guglielmo Marconi first seriously tested wireless telegraphy. He made his historic transmission between here and ★**Rathlin Island** ❻, 13 km (8 miles) off the coast towards Scotland. The boomerang-shaped island, whose population has slumped from 2,000 to 100 since 1850, attracts geologists, botanists and birdwatchers; a reserve (tel: 2076 3948) monitors an estimated 250,000 birds of 175 species. There is one pub a hotel, guesthouse and youth hostel – but no policeman, and no need for one. A ferry (tel: 2076 9299) makes the journey in 50

Map
on pages
80–81

*Below: the Carrick-a-Rede
Rope Bridge
Bottom: the Giant's Causeway*

minutes and a minibus tours the island in summer. Advance booking required (tel: Puffin Tours: 2076 3451 or 077 528 61788).

Eight km (5 miles) west, off the A2, is the **★Carrick-a-rede Rope Bridge** (Mar–Oct, tel: 2076 9839, car park, fee), swinging precariously over a 24-metre (80-ft) chasm to an island salmon fishery. It's worth crossing the bridge for the view. Past Whitepark Bay is **Dunseverick Castle,** the slight remains of a 6th-century fortress perched on a high crag overlooking a fishing harbour.

THE GIANT'S CAUSEWAY

The castle is at the eastern end of the **★★★Giant's Causeway 7**, an astonishing assembly, discovered only in 1692, of more than 40,000 basalt columns, mostly perfect hexagonals formed by the cooling of molten lava. Dr Samuel Johnson, when asked by his biographer James Boswell whether this wonder of the world was worth seeing, gave the immortal reply: "Worth seeing? yes; but not worth going to see." It was a shrewd judgment in the 1770s when roads in the region were primitive.

Today this geological curiosity is accessible to the most monstrous tourist coaches, but it can still disappoint some visitors, who expect the columns to be bigger (the tallest, in the **Giant's Organ**, are about 12 metres/39 ft) or who find their regularity diminishes their magnificence. It remains worth seeing, though. The formal approach is via the Causeway Centre (Causeway Head, tel: 2073 1855, car park fee) 3 km (2 miles) north of Bushmills on the B146. A minibus provides wheelchair access to the Causeway.

One of the most pleasant ways to reach the Giant's

Causeway from Bushmills is on the **Giant's Causeway and Bushmills Railway steam train**, which operates daily July, August and Easter (weekends March–Oct), fee.

THE WORLD'S OLDEST DISTILLERY

The distillery at ★★**Bushmills ⑧** (Distillery Road, tel: 2073 3218. Guided tours daily, www.bushmills.com) a couple of miles away, boasts the world's oldest whiskey-making licence (1608). Old Bushmills, Black Bush and Bushmills Malt, made from local barley and the water that flows by in St Columb's Rill, can be tasted after a tour. Connoisseurs tend to prefer the classic Black Bush to the more touted (and expensive) malt. The main difference between Scotch whisky and Irish whiskey, apart from the spelling, is that Scotch is distilled twice and Irish three times.

About 3 km (2 miles) along the coast road are the romantic remains of ★★**Dunluce Castle** (tel: 2073 1938, closed Mon and Sun am). Poised on a rocky headland besides sheer cliffs, the 14th-century stronghold is immense and dramatic. The novelist William Makepeace Thackeray wrote of "those grey towers of Dunluce standing upon a leaden rock and looking as if some old old princess of old old fairy times were dragon guarded within." It was abandoned in 1641, two years after part of the kitchen collapsed into the sea during a storm, carrying many of the servants to their death. In the graveyard of the adjacent ruined church are buried sailors from the Spanish Armada galleass *Girona*, which was wrecked on nearby rocks in 1588 with 1,300 men on board and was located on the seabed in 1967. Many of the *Girona*'s treasures are in the Ulster Museum, Belfast.

PORTRUSH AND PORTSTEWART

Next along the coast are two seaside resorts. **Portrush ⑨** is the brasher, tackier, offering amusement arcades, burger bars, karaoke pubs, souvenir shops, guest-houses, a children's adventure play park, boats trips for sea fishing and viewing the Causeway, and two championship golf courses. The **Dunluce Centre** (7082 4444, admission fee, May–Aug daily; Sept–Oct weekends only; Nov–Apr closed, offers virtual-reality 'Treasure Fortress'). **Portrush Countryside Centre** (Bath Road, tel: 7082 3600, free, closed Oct–Mar) has rock pool animals in a touch tank.

Portstewart is the quieter, a tidy Victorian town with a huge strand, excellent for beach casting but plagued by speeding cars which, unaccountably, are allowed free

Star Attractions
● **Giant's Causeway**
● **Bushmills Distillery**
● **Dunluce Castle**

Below: Bushmills Inn
Middle: Dunluce Castle
Bottom: Portstewart harbour

Map
on pages
80–81

Below: Mussenden Temple
Middle: Clotworthy Gardens
Bottom: a day at the beach

access. Long-distance walkers can pick up the **North Antrim Coast Path** at Portstewart Strand; it forms part of the Ulster Way and extends eastwards for 64 km (40 miles) to **Murlough Bay**.

Nearby **Coleraine**, built for 18th-century planters, is a busy but ordinary market and university town.

A CHOICE OF ROUTES

Here, you can either continue westwards towards Derry City or proceed south towards Belfast.

Along the first choice, the A2 towards Derry City, on a windswept headland at **Downhill** ⓾, the massive roofless ruin of **Downhill Castle** (1780) dominates the skyline. Its ★**Mussenden Temple** (Mussenden Road, Castlerock, tel: 7084 8728, free; 13 Jun–Aug daily; Apr, May and Sept weekends only; Oct–Mar closed), is perched precariously near a 60-metre (200-ft) cliff and housed an eccentric bishop's library and possibly his mistress; it was inspired by the temples of Vesta at Tivoli and Rome. **Downhill Forest** has lovely walks, a fish pond and waterfalls.

Benone Beach, part of Magilligan Strand, is one of Ireland's best, with golf, tennis, heated pools and children's play areas available at its excellent adjoining Tourist Complex (tel: 7775 0555). At the beginning of the strand is a famous **Martello Tower**, built in 1812 to defend the coast during the Napoleonic wars.

The second route takes you close to **Antrim** town ⓫, with its Lough Neagh summer cruises, its 10th-century round tower and its **Clotworthy Gardens** (open daylight hours). The gardens were laid out by André Le Nôtre, who created those at Versailles for Louis XIV.

Derry City

Derry ⑫ is famously friendly. Even in its sectarian squabbles, it is far less implacable than Belfast. The 19th-century Scottish historian Thomas Carlyle called it "the prettiest looking town I have seen in Ireland" and, though the Troubles seriously scarred it, recent refurbishment has restored its attractiveness. But the city, finely situated on the **River Foyle**, doesn't set out to be a calendar girl; it prefers to provide exhilarating company, and it succeeds. Community activities and the arts are strong here.

The city's growth was financed by London guilds, which in 1614 began creating the last walled city in Europe. Its purpose was mercantile success and you can still see traces of its former economic confidence in the ornamental facades of the old shirtmaking factories, which provided the city with its livelihood for generations. The ★★**walls**, 6m (20 ft) thick and complete with watch-towers and cannon such as the 18-pounder **Roaring Meg ⓐ** (dating from 1642), are marvellously intact. (For fee-paying tours, tel: 7134 7176; otherwise free access.)

Two 17th-century sieges failed to breach the walls, earning the sobriquet "maiden city". Some say the city still has a siege mentality, a theory reinforced by the IRA's daubed slogan "You are now entering Free Derry." This was the name given to the **Bogside ⓑ**, a densely populated Roman Catholic housing estate, when its inhabitants barricaded it against the police in 1969. Their grievances were old ones. After Ireland's partition in 1920, the city's governing Unionists had fixed constituency boundaries to ensure a "permanent" majority for themselves in what was a mainly nationalist area – an artificial majority that wasn't overturned until the mid-1970s. Feeling isolated from the prosperous eastern counties, Derry's citizens built up both a wonderful community spirit and a resentment that finally boiled over.

The most famous siege took place in 1689, when the Catholic forces of James II, the last of England's Stuart kings, blockaded the Protestant supporters of William of Orange for 15 weeks, almost forcing them into sub-mission. About 7,000 of the 30,000 people packed within the city's walls died of disease or starvation. One member of the besieged garrison chillingly recorded the selling prices of horseflesh, dogs' heads, cats, and rats "fattened by eating the bodies of the slain Irish."

The city's eventual relief is depicted on the siege memorial window of ★**St Columb's Cathedral ⓒ** (London Street, tel: 7126 7313, admission fee) a graceful

★

Star Attraction
● **Derry's walls**

Below: Derry's Guildhall
Bottom: the symbolic 'Hands Across the Divide' sculpture by Maurice Harron

Maps:
Area 80
City 90

Remembering Amelia

The Earhart Centre 2.5 km (1½ miles) north-west on B194 (Ballyarnet, tel: 028-7135 4040, free) focuses on a famous date in aviation – the day Amelia Earhart, the first woman to fly solo across the Atlantic, landed here in 1932.

The Tower Museum

17th-century Anglican church built in "Planters' Gothic" style. The chapter house contains siege relics. Outside the walls, off Bishop Street Without, the **Church of St Columb** (tel: 7126 2301, admission free), built 1784, known as the Long Tower Church, has a lavish interior.

For those interested in the city's turbulent history, the award-winning **★Tower Museum** (Union Hall Place, tel: 7137 2411, closed Sun and Mon, except July–Aug, open daily) skilfully uses audio-visuals and photography to tell its story from both sides of the sectarian divide. An exhibition tells the story of *La Trinidad Valencera*, a Spanish Armada ship lost off the Donegal coast in 1588.

The innovative **Nerve Centre ❶** (7 Magazine Street, tel: 7126 0652) hosts live music and various arts activities.

Streets from the city's original four gates (Shipquay, Ferryquay, Bishop's and Butcher's) converge on **The Diamond**, a perversely square-shaped market place at the top of Shipquay Street, the steepest main thoroughfare in Ireland. At the bottom of the street, the **Guildhall ❷** (Guildhall Place, tel: 7137 7335, admission free, closed weekends and bank holidays), one of those Tudor-Gothic structures popular in Northern Ireland, clearly shows the influence of the London merchants.

Behind the Guildhall is **Derry Quay**, celebrated in song by hundreds of thousands of emigrants who sailed down the Foyle from here, bound for a new life in America. The city's maritime past is covered in the **Harbour Museum ❸** (Harbour Square, tel: 7137 7331, admission free, closed weekends); displays include a replica of a 9-m (30-ft) curragh in which St Columba sailed to Iona in AD563.

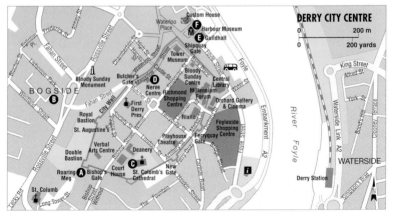

Donegal

The most northerly point in Ireland is not in Northern Ireland but in the Republic, just across the border from Derry in County Donegal. It's an open, unspoiled region, popular with holidaymakers.

Bundoran ⓭ is a brash resort, kiss-me-quick and windy. **Rossnowlagh**, its smaller quieter cousin, is a base for surfers. In the one-time garrison town of **Ballyshannon**, the waters of the Erne are tamed to produce hydro-electricty, and pretty Georgian houses survive.

Donegal ⓮, the lively county town, has a busy triangular "Diamond" market square, congested with tourist traffic all summer. The town's **castle** (07497-22405, admission fee, open all year), once an O'Donnell stronghold, was redesigned, as was the town, by the Brookes, planters who took over the land 400 years ago.

Five km (3 miles) south of Donegal town, at Laghy, the R232 runs south-east for Pettigoe from where the R233 bears north 5 km (3 miles) across desolate bogland to **Lough Derg**, with its tiny **Station Island**, focal point for a major act of pilgrimage, St Patrick's Purgatory.

Glencolumbkille ⓯, further west, pioneered the idea that the draughty, cold traditional thatched white-washed cottage could be up-graded, given central heating, pine furniture, shower, TV set and fridge and clustered into a marketable group. Three cottages in the village's **Folk Village Museum** (07497-30017, admission fee, closed Oct–Easter) present traditional rural life.

TORY ISLAND

From **Burtonport**, a 25-minute ferry service (07495-20532) runs to **Aranmore** island 5 km (3 miles) offshore, with its 900 souls, dry stone walls and holiday cottages. Ferries for bare and windswept **Tory Island**, now a popular tourist destination, run the 24-km (15-mile) sea journey from **Bunbeg** and from **Meenlaragh** round the **Bloody Foreland** near Gortahork. The Irish-speaking island's main village, West Town, has a 15-m (51-ft) round tower and the ruins of two churches.

Thirty-seven km (21 miles) north on the N56, **Dunfanaghy**'s fame rests on its popularity with Northern Ireland's golfers).

Letterkenny ⓰ is situated on the River Swilly 16 km (10 miles) to the southwest. Its most prominent landmark is the Cathedral, built in modern Gothic style by local masons using Donegal stone.

Below: Dildooney More dolmen
Bottom: Doon fort

Map
on pages
80–81

Tyrone

Strabane – Sion Mills – Omagh – Ulster-American Folk Park – Dungannon – Draperstown – Cookstown

Twenty-one km (13 miles) southwest of Derry City, in county Tyrone on the A5, is **Strabane ⓱**, a border town paired with Lifford on the Donegal side. John Dunlap, printer of America's Declaration of Independence, learned his trade in **Gray's Printing Press** (49 Main Street, tel: 7188 4094, museum free, Tues–Sat, all year; admission fee to National Trust section, Apr–Sept Tues–Sat pm only). In **Dergalt**, 3 km (2 miles) to the southeast, signposted off the B47, is a whitewashed cottage, the ancestral home of US president Woodrow Wilson (tel: 7138 4444, open Jul–Aug pm only, fee).

Sion Mills, 3 miles (5 km) south of Strabane, is a village whose name betrays its origins. The linen-workers' old cottages are charming. The Parish Church of the Good Shepherd is a striking Italian-style edifice, contrasting sharply with the modern architecture of St Teresa's Catholic Church, whose facade displays a large image on slate of the Last Supper.

As you drive into **Omagh ⓲**, the county town of Tyrone, 25 km (16 miles) along the A5, the religious fragmentation of Northern Ireland is apparent in the abundance of churches. The joining of the Rivers Camowen and Drumragh to form the Strule make the location pleasant enough, but Omagh is more a town for living (and praying) in than for visiting. Locals still recall the Saturday afternoon in August 1998 when a maroon Vauxhall Astra exploded in the town, killing 29 people.

ULSTER-AMERICAN FOLK PARK

Thomas Mellon, who emigrated to Pittsburgh at the age of five in 1818, went on to found a great industrial and banking empire. His descendants, having traced their family roots to 6 km (4 miles) north of Omagh, off the A5, endowed the **★★Ulster-American Folk Park ⓳** on the site at Camphill (tel: 8224 3292, admission fee, Apr–Sept Mon–Sat 10.30am–6pm, Sun 11am–5pm; Oct–Mar Mon–Fri 10.30am–5pm).

Thomas Mellon's boyhood home forms the centrepiece of the award-winning park. To illuminate the transition made by the 18th-century emigrants, craftsmen's cottages, a schoolhouse, a blacksmith's forge and a Presbyterian meeting-house from the Old World have been rebuilt on

American connections

During tough times in the 1800s, the area's strong Scots-Presbyterian work ethic spurred many to seek their fortune in America. The results were remarkable and Northern Ireland claims that 11 US presidents have had roots in the province: Andrew Jackson, James Knox Polk, Andrew Johnson, James Buchanan, Ulysses S. Grant, Chester Alan Arthur, Grover Cleveland, Benjamin Harrison, William McKinley, Theodore Roosevelt and Woodrow Wilson. Genealogists pore over old documents, hoping to add more names, and many Americans visit to seek out ancestral homes.

The Sperrins landscape

a peat bog alongside log cabins, a Pennsylvania farmstead and a covered wagon from the New World. Peat is kept burning in the cottages, and there are demonstrations of candle-making, fish-salting and horse-shoeing.

An indoor exhibit recreates the main street of an Ulster town 100 years ago, its hardware shop displaying foot warmers and lamp wicks, its medical hall containing Bishop's Granular Effervescent Citrate of Magnesia and Belladonna breast plasters. A replica of an emigrant ship links the continents. There's not a whiff of Disney, thanks to the attention to detail, though the American "half" looks more prosperous than the original settlers would have found it.

A **Centre for Migration Studies** on the site has a reference library open to the public for research.

RELICS OF OLD INDUSTRIES

There's nothing Northern Ireland likes better than history, and almost every village in Tyrone – **Castlederg, Creggan, Donaghmore, Fivemiletown, Newtown-stewart** – has its heritage centre. Along the A505 from Omagh, **An Creagan Visitor Centre** in **Creggan** (tel: 8076 1112, free entry), at the foothills to the Sperrin Mountains, hosts an interpretative exhibition of the area; it also has a crafts shop, bar, self-catering cottages and regular cultural events.

With the eclipse of Ulster's once-flourishing linen industry, hard times have again come to villages such as **Draperstown** (built in 1618 by the London Company of Drapers) in the archaeologically rich, blue-tinged **Sperrin Mountains**. Near **Maghera**, a working linen mill (Wm. Clark and Sons, Upperlands, tel: 7954 7200) may be

Star Attraction
● **Ulster-American Folk Park**

The Ulster-American Folk Park recreates old streets (below) and has rebuilt the Mellon homestead (bottom)

Map on pages 80–81

Map on pages 80–81

Heaney tribute

The poet Seamus Heaney, a Nobel Laureate, is celebrated near his native village (Heaney Library, Bellaghy Bawn, Bellaghy, tel: 028-7938 6812, open Mon–Sat Easter–Sept 10am–6pm, Oct–Easter 9am–5pm, admission fee). Much of Heaney's poetry derives its intense imagery and colloquial language from his rural upbringing in this part of Northern Ireland.

Walking in the Sperrins

visited by arrangement. The fortunes of towns like **Dungannon ㉑**, 21 km (13 miles) south of Cookstown and once the seat of the great O'Neill clan, have faltered too. On the A45 Coalisland Road out of town, **Tyrone Crystal** runs factory tours Mon–Fri (tel: 8772 5335 for times; fee).

Signposted from the M1 motorway, exit 13, 11 km (7 miles) east of Dungannon, is the always open **Peatlands Park** (Peatlands Park Centre and Railway, tel: 3885 1102, fee for a miniature railway which is closed Sept–Easter Sun), a unique preservation of an Irish bog's flora and fauna which can be viewed from the railway carriages.

COOKSTOWN

Forty km (25 miles) east of Omagh, **Cookstown ㉒**, the exact middle of Northern Ireland, is renowned for its main street, 3 km (2 miles) long and 50m (160 ft) wide, and can be located from miles away by the 61-m (200-ft) spire of the Gothic-style Catholic church. The town (population 6,700) has a strong tradition of nationalism, often refined in its many old-fashioned pubs.

Just east of the town an 18-hole golf course (200 Killymoon Rd., tel: 8676 3762) occupies the grounds of **Killymoon Castle**, designed in 1803 by John Nash, architect of London's Regent Street. Some years ago, a farmer bought the castle, then derelict, for £100.

Many Neolithic graves and stone circles are sprinkled around both towns. The best are at **Beaghmore** (free access), 16 km (10 miles) west of Cookstown, off the A53. Villages such as **Clogher** and **Coagh**, **Moneymore** and **Pomeroy** are noted for fine traditional musicians and a variety of ecclesiastical architecture.

Fermanagh's lakeland

Enniskillen – Devenish Island – Boa Island – Lough Derg – Belleek – Marble Arch Caves – Florence Court

The county town, **Enniskillen ㉓**, a Protestant stronghold since Tudor times, is built on an island between two channels of the River Erne as it flows from **Upper** to **Lower Lough Erne**. In summer, pleasure boats ply (MV *Kestrel*, Round O Jetty, tel: 6632 2882, May and June Sun; July and Aug daily; Sept Tues and weekends) the lakes, and western Europeans cruise them in hired craft (Manor House Marine, Killadeas, tel: 6862 8100).

The town's strategic importance is shown by **Enniskillen Castle** (Castle Barracks, tel: 6632 5000, admission fee, closed Sat, Sun and Mon am, open May– Jun & Sept Mon–Sat; July and Aug daily; Oct–Apr Mon–Fri) the earliest parts dating from the 15th century. The castle has two museums, one focusing on prehistory, the other on military relics.

Enniskillen is rich in small bakeries and butcher's shops, and there's a gossipy atmosphere as farmers mix with townsfolk in Blakes of the Hollow, one of the North's finest pubs. A secret is soon shared in such a place. There's a good view from the head of the 108 stairs of **Cole's Monument** (Forthill Park, tel: 6632 3110, admission fee, open Apr–Sept 1.30–3pm).

DEVENISH ISLAND

A true taste of the region's flavour can be gained by circling Lower Lough Erne by road or by boat. **★Devenish Island ㉔** is reached by ferry (boat fare and admission fee, accessible daily Apr–Sept) from Trory Point, signposted 5 km (3 miles) north of the town at the A32/B82 junction. It is the best known of the lough's 97 islands because of its elaborate and well-preserved round tower, which can be climbed by internal ladders. Close by are the decorative ruins of the 12th-century Augustinian Abbey of St Mary.

Five km (3 miles) south of Kesh on the B82, along the lough's north shore, a ferry departs (Castle Archdale Park Marina, tel: 6862 1156, ferry fare, admission free, Easter and June–Sept only except Mondays) for **★White Island** with its 12th-century church along one wall of which are lined up eight mysterious pagan statues. Their origins fox experts; some speculate that seven may represent the deadly sins.

Below: canoeing on Lough Erne at Enniskillen
Bottom: ancient monuments on Devenish Island

Map on pages 80–81

Below: Boa Island's Janus
Bottom: Florence Court

ANCIENT MONUMENTS

A few miles further, past the village of **Kesh**, is the strangest of all the ancient stone figures: the two-faced Janus statue on ★★**Boa Island** ㉕, which is joined to the mainland by a bridge at each end. Watch for an easily missable road sign pointing to "Caldragh Cemetery" (free access), then tramp down a farm lane until you find, in the middle of a field, an inscrutable Celtic figure. The figure's sexual arousal and the hollow in its head suggest that hollow may once have held sacrificial blood.

A second Janus figure was discovered on the little island of **Lustybeg**, near Kesh. There are holiday chalets for hire on this island.

Following the lough's shoreline, you reach **Pettigoe**, an old plantation town once the railhead for pilgrims visiting the holy sites at **Lough Derg,** across the border in Co. Donegal. The River Termon, running through Pettigoe, marks the border and is said to be stuffed full of bilingual trout. An oak tree on one side of the bridge was planted in 1853 to mark the British victory at Sebastopol. A statue on the other side commemorates four IRA men who died fighting the British in 1922.

Castle Caldwell, on the A47 6 km (4 miles) east of Belleek, a ruined 16th-century castle by the loughside nearby, has become the centrepiece of a Forest Park (details tel: 6863 1253, free access, daily dawn to dusk), popular with picnickers and bird watchers. Worth seeing is a "Fermanagh cot", a 9-m (30-ft) wooden barge used for transporting cattle and sheep to and from the islands of Upper and Lower Lough Erne.

BELLEEK

The border touches the River Erne again at ★★**Belleek** ㉖, where anglers assure you that you can hook a salmon in the Republic and land it in Northern Ireland. The village is famous for its lustrous and intricate **Belleek pottery**, manufactured from felspar imported from Norway. Half-hour tours (Belleek Pottery, tel: 6865 9300, www.belleek.ie, admission free; Sept–Apr Mon–Fri) of the working factory (established 1857) are available. The pottery's Visitor Centre, where the products are on sale, opens Mon–Fri all year and daily Mar–Oct.

You can take the scenic drive back to Enniskillen along the south side of the lough, stopping 8 km (5 miles) north-west of Derrygonnelly on the A46 at **Lough Navar Forest Park** (details 6864 1256, free access, daily dawn to dusk, restricted access for cars). Here, a lookout point offers a panorama of five counties. At **Tully**, off the A46, 5 km (3 miles) north of the village, is one well-preserved 17th-century castle (admission fee, open Tues–Sat, Apr–Sept) whilst at **Monea**, 11 km (7 miles) north-west of Enniskillen on the B81, is another castle with free access at all times.

MARBLE ARCH CAVES

"Over 300 million years of history" – impressive even by Irish standards – is the slogan used to promote ★★**Marble Arch Caves** ㉗ (Marlbank Scenic Loop, Florencecourt, tel: 6634 8855, admission fee, accessible Mar–Sept, weather permitting), an extensive network of limestone chambers, containing remarkable stalactites. A 75-minute tour includes an underground boat journey. The "Moses Walk" is so called because the dammed walkway has been created through a lake, with more than a metre of water on either side. There's a café and shop.

Located 20 km (12 miles) south-west of Enniskillen, the caves are reached by following the A4 southwest for 5 km (3 miles), then following signposts after branching off on the A32 towards Swanlinbar.

FLORENCE COURT

★**Florence Court** (National Trust, tel: 6634 8249, admission fee, closed Oct–Mar, as well as Tues and mornings all year; open weekends only during May and Sept), is a beautiful 18th-century mansion 6 km (4 miles) back. Contents include fine rococo plasterwork and 18th-century furniture. The grounds include an ice house, a water-powered sawmill and a walled garden.

Star Attractions
● **Boa Island**
● **Belleek**
● **Marble Arch Caves**

Castle Coole
Three km (2 miles) southeast of Enniskillen on the A4 is Ireland's finest classical mansion, Castle Coole (National Trust, tel: 6632 2690, admission fee, closed Oct–Mar; open Apr, May, Sept weekends and by appointment; Jun–Aug Fri–Wed). Completed in 1798, it is a perfect example of late 18th-century Hellenism and has furniture dating from before 1830. The park lake's flock of graylag geese was established here 300 years ago.

Why fishermen come to Fermanagh

Map
on pages
80–81

Armagh's two St Patrick's cathedrals: the Roman Catholic one (below) and the Protestant version (bottom)

Armagh

Armagh City – Crossmaglen – Portadown – Lurgan

County Armagh is traditionally known as the Apple Orchard of Ireland. Its county town of **Armagh** ㉘ (always called a city despite a population of just 15,000) symbolises many of Northern Ireland's problems. Its two striking cathedrals – one Protestant, one Catholic, both called **St Patrick's** – sit on opposite hills like, someone once said, the horns of a dilemma (the dilemma being how to get the two communities to live together in harmony).

Armagh is known for its dignified Georgian architecture. At one end of an oval **Mall** – where cricket is played in summer – is a classical courthouse, at the other a former jailhouse. The Ionic-pillared ★**County Museum** (The Mall, tel: 3752 3070, admission free, closed Sun) contains local artifacts and collections on military history and railways.

Access is free into the ordered gardens of the 1790 **Observatory** which also accommodate Ireland's only ★★**Planetarium** (College Hill, tel: 3752 3689.) Astronomical shows have been enhanced by a major refurbishment to the Digital Theatre, including the world's most advanced digital projection system. There are also interactive exhibitions and an outdoor Astropark with scale models of the planets. It also hosts regular activities.

Three km (2 miles) west of the city, off the A28, is the high-tech ★**Navan Centre** (tel: 3752 1801, Easter–June weekdays, Jul–Aug daily, closed in winter, admission fee for exhibition, free into site), celebrating Emain Macha, Ulster's Camelot around 600BC. Until recent restorations,

it was a neglected hilltop; now it comes complete with hands-on computers and audio-visual interpretation facilities. Access to the hilltop itself is free.

The **Palace Stables Heritage Centre** (tel: 3752 9629, Friary Road, admission fee, Easter–Jun weekdays, Jul–Aug daily), past the ruins of a 13th-century friary, at the former archbishop's palace, recreates the building's daily life in 1786. In the city centre **St Patrick's Trian** (40 English Street, tel: 3752 1801, admission fee for exhibition, Mon–Sat 10am–5pm, Sun 1–5pm) relates the city's history and its connections with St Patrick. A 20-ft (6-m) giant relates the adventures of Dean Swift's Gulliver.

NEAT VILLAGES

The city is surrounded by neat villages, reached through a network of pleasant lanes. Each May, the countryside around **Loughgall** is radiant with apple blossom. In the village the **Dan Winter Ancestral Home** (9 The Diamond, Derryloughan Road, tel: 3885 1344, admission free, open daily, Sun pm only) displays details of the founding of the Orange Order. Near **Markethill**, in **Gosford Forest Park** (tel: 3755 1277, admission fee, closes at dusk), Gosford Castle is a large turreted mock-Norman edifice built of local granite.

Crossmaglen has a remarkably large market square, containing a bronze monument to the IRA; this village was in the front line of battles between the IRA and the security forces. Remarkably, after enduring many bloody sectarian murders, Crossmaglen began promoting tourism with some success in the 1990s. On the B30, 13 km (8 miles) towards Camlough, the thatched **Mullaghbawn Folk Museum** (tel: 3088 8278, admission fee, tours by appointment only) preserves a traditional farmhouse.

CRAIGAVON

Between Armagh and Belfast is a chain of towns built on commerce. **Portadown ㉙**, 16 km (10 miles) to the northeast, has found its role scaled down from that of a major railway junction to a prosperous market town noted for rose growing and coarse fishing. Linen manufacturing has diminished, as it has in **Lurgan**, 10 km (6 miles) further along the A3. In the 1960s it was decided to link the two towns to form the "lineal city" of **Craigavon**, thereby reducing congestion in Belfast; but civic pride has kept the separate identities of Portadown and Lurgan very much alive despite the mushrooming between them of housing estates, schools and countless traffic circles.

Star Attraction
● **Armagh Planetarium**

Lough Neagh
Lough Neagh (pronounced *Nay*), 27 km long and 18 km wide (17 by 11 miles) is the largest inland sheet of water in the British Isles. Legend has it that the warrior giant Finn McCool created the lake by scooping up a mighty handful of earth to fling at a rival Scottish giant (he missed, and the rock and clay fell into the Irish Sea to create the Isle of Man). Because of the lough's marshy edges, it has surprisingly few access points – one reason why it has remained one of western Europe's most important bird habitats. The Lough Neagh Discovery Centre on Oxford Island (Mon–Fri 9am–5pm, Sat–Sun 10am–5pm, open until 6pm Easter–Sept) runs audio-visual shows about the wildlife and has a gift shop and café. Recreational facilities for sailing and water-skiing have been developed, with marinas at Oxford Island (south shore) and Ballyronan (west shore).

Georgian architecture on The Mall, Armagh

Map on pages 80–81

Downpatrick and the Mournes

Downpatrick – Ardglass – Mourne Mountains – Newcastle – Kilkeel – Rostrevor – Warrenpoint

Moody Mournes

The Mournes are "young" mountains (like the Alps) and their chameleon qualities attract walkers. One moment the granite is grey, the next pink. You walk by an isolated farmhouse, and within moments are in the middle of a wilderness. One minute, the Mournes justify all the songs written about them; the next, they become plain scrubland and un-exceptional hills. The weather has a lot to do with this variety.

Downpatrick ③⓪, whose name is a marriage of Patrick, this island's patron saint and apostle, and the Irish for fort (*dún*) is 14 km (22 miles) to the southeast of Belfast via the A7. The son of a Roman official in Wales, Patrick sailed up Stangford Lough and the Quoile to Saul where he built his first church. Patrick's remains may lie under the **★gravestone** marked with his name at Downpatrick's Protestant **★★Cathedral Church of the Holy and Undivided Trinity**, or they may lie under the church itself.

You can follow Patrick's story in a superb interactive exhibition at the **St Patrick Centre** (Lower Market St, tel: 4461 9000, open daily, Sun Oct–March open on request). The centre is the hub of Downpatrick's week of celebrations around St Patrick's Day, 17 March. Some people picnic 3 km (1¾ miles) east by the healing waters of the bath-houses at Struell's **St Patrick's Wells**. Others, a mile northwest, contemplate the 1180 Cistercian **Inch Abbey** ruins (admission charge). Occasional steam trains run to the abbey from the town's railway station (www.downrail.co.uk).

Further attractions in Downpatrick itself include the **★Down County Museum** (Jun–Aug, Mon–Fri 11am–5pm, weekend 2–5pm; rest of year Tues–Fri 11–5pm, Sat 2–5pm) in the 1789 jailhouse, complete with cells.

ARDGLASS

Southeast of Downpatrick, **Ardglass**'s herring port is proud of its marina and seven castles. Yawls from picturesque **Killough**, just to the south, once traded brandy from Bordeaux and timber from Trondheim. Along the coast past Clough's Norman ruin, sleepy **Dundrum** has a fine 12th-century **★Norman castle** (Apr–Sept, Tues–Sat 9am–6pm, Sunday 1–6pm; Oct–Mar Sat 10am–4pm, Sun 2–4pm).

MOUTAINS OF MOURNE

Then comes the Victorian resort of **Newcastle ③①** where the compact but steep **★★★Mountains of Mourne** do, as the Percy French ballad describes, 'run down to the sea'. Here, the Royal County Down links is rated in the world's top 20 golf courses. The town, which has a fine, sandy beach, tries for amusement arcade jollity, but is too small and picturesque to be truly vulgar. The Mourne range peaks at Slieve Donard's 852m (2,796 ft) and is relieved by the

St Patrick's gravestone in Downpatrick – though few scholars believe he is actually buried there

Castlewellan and **Tollymore** Forest Parks – good for riding (pony or bicycle) or walking.

The B27, which runs north from **Kilkeel**, affords fine views of the Mournes before continuing to Belfast through **Banbridge**, with its polar bear memorial to Captain Crozier, discoverer of the North West Passage, and its **Brontë Trail** commemorating a local schoolmaster, Patrick, father of the novelists Charlotte, Emily and Anne.

In the direction of Belfast, just off the A1, **Hillsborough**, packed with antique shops and English-style pubs, is rich in Georgian architecture. **Lisburn** ㉜ has an informative **Museum** and ★**Irish Linen Centre** (Mon–Sat 9.30am– 5pm). Fast water rides are popular in the multi-pool **Lagan Valley LeisurePlex** (Governors Road, tel: 9267 2121).

SEASIDE RESORTS

An alternative route loops south of the Mournes, west along the coast from Kilkeel past formidable 13th-century **Greencastle**. It takes in bosky ★**Rostrevor** ㉝ with its obelisk to the English Major-General Robert Ross who stormed the White House in 1814, scoffing President Madison's abandoned dinner.

A steep half-mile walk up the slopes of **Slievemartin** (486m/1,595 ft) brings you to **Cloghmore**, a "Big Stone" supposedly hurled by the Irish giant Fionn MacCool at a rival Scot. The geological explanation for this misplaced piece of granite is more mundane, relating to glacial drift.

Beyond is breezy **Warrenpoint**, which has two piers (good for fishing), a spacious square and a half-mile prom-enade. **Narrow Water Castle**, built in 1560, has a grue-some murder hole (Jul–Sept 11am–4.30pm, closed Wed).

Star Attractions
● **Downpatrick**
● **Mourne Mountains**

Below: riding out at Newcastle
Bottom: where the Mountains of Mourne sweep down to the sea

Map on pages 80–81

Strangford's wildlife

The lough, one of Europe's most important wildlife sites, has more than 2,000 species of marine animal. Its wetlands support 25,000 wildfowl and 50,000 waders. Several varieties of tern arrive in summer, and in winter the lough is thought to support 75 percent of the world's Brent geese. Ireland's largest colony of common seals breeds here, and 9-metre (30-ft) basking sharks are sometimes seen in the lough's entrance.

Inside Exploris

Ards Peninsula & the Gold Coast

Comber – Strangford Lough – Exploris – Greyabbey – Newtownards – Donaghadee – Bangor – Holywood

Comber ㉞, 14 km (9 miles) to the southeast of Belfast at the head of Strangford Lough, was a linen town and still has a working mill. The town centre retains its old character, despite the developers, with single-storey cottage shops and a square. **Castle Espie** (Wildfowl and Wetlands Trust, 78 Ballydrain Road, tel: 9187 4146, admission fee) is base for Ireland's largest collection of ducks, geese and swans.

Strangford Lough, an environmental conservation area, is noted for its myriad islands, most of which are sunken drumlins, the smooth glacial hillocks which characterise the Co. Down rolling landscape. There are rocky shores on this side of the lough at places like **Whiterock Bay**. **Mahee Island**, accessible by a bridge, has a golf course and the remains of an early monastery, **Nendrum Abbey**, destroyed by the Vikings in 974AD (free access to site always, museum fee, closed Monday).

STRANGFORD

You can reach the **Ards Peninsula**, a 37-km (23-mile) long finger dotted with villages and beaches, by means of a regular car ferry which chugs a slanted course from ★**Strangford** ㉟, 13 km (8 miles) from Downpatrick, across to Portaferry. The Vikings are said to have had a trading post at Strangford in the 9th century.

Nearby is **Castle Ward House** (tel: 4488 1204, admission fee, open daily Jul–Aug and weekends only Mar–Jun & Sept–Oct; closed Nov–early Mar), an 18th-century Georgian mansion, once the home of the Lord of Bangor. Overlooking the lough, the house has two "fronts" in differing styles (classical and gothic) because the Lord and his Lady had diverging tastes. There are wildfowl in the 280-hectare (700-acre) grounds and the ★**Strangford Lough Wildlife Centre** is located at the water's edge. There's also a Victorian laundry, two small 15th-century castles and an adventure playground for children.

The ferry across the mouth of the lough deposits you where the sunsets and the local lobster are memorable. ★★**Exploris** (Castle Street, Portaferry, tel: 4272 8062, admission fee, closed Sun am), Northern Ireland's only sea aquarium and seal sanctuary, examines many of the 2,000-plus sea creatures to be found in the lough.

Fourteen km (9 miles) north of Portaferry along the A20 is the one-street town of **Kircubbin**, a boating centre with a small pier jutting into Strangford Lough. Three km (2 miles) inland takes you to the **Kirkistown Circuit**, a wartime airport and the home of car racing in Northern Ireland. Motor sport has a keen following in Northern Ireland; motorcycle racing and rallying can take place on public roads closed by Act of Parliament for the events.

Six km (4 miles) further north on the A20 in the pretty village of **Greyabbey** is the site, with "physick garden", of an 1193 Cistercian abbey, and one of the most complete of its type in Ireland (tel: 4278 8585, free admission, open Apr–Sep Tues–Sat 9am–6pm and Sun 2–7pm).

MOUNT STEWART

Three km (2 miles) north of the village is another National Trust treasure, ★★**Mount Stewart** ❸ (tel: 4278 8387, admission fee; gardens open daily all year; house open Mar–Oct, call for times). It is an 18th-century house which has several fine gardens and a mild microclimate which fosters delicate plants untypical of the area. The rhododendrons are particularly fine, and the gardens contain a variety of statues of griffins, satyrs, heraldic lions and the like. Mountstewart House was the birthplace of Lord Castlereagh, England's foreign secretary during the Napoleonic Wars. The **Temple of the Winds**, an 18th-century folly in the grounds, was built by James Stewart, a rival of Robert Adam, and is modelled on another in Athens. It offers a splendid view of the lough.

Newtownards ❸, a sprawling commuter town at the head of Strangford Lough, belies its name; it's an old

Below: Greyabbey ruins
Bottom: Mount Stewart

Map
on pages
80–81

*Below: Donaghadee harbour
Bottom: the 18th-century
Ballycopeland Windmill*

market town, dating back to the 17th century. Today it's a bustling shopping centre with a blend of traditional shops and a covered shopping centre. There is a fine sandstone town hall and other buildings of historical interest include **Movilla Abbey** on the site of a 6th-century monastery about a mile to the east of the town. The airfield, a centre for amateur fliers (Ulster Flying Club, tel: 9181 3327), stages a spectacular annual display of aerobatics.

The **Somme Heritage Centre** (233 Bangor Road, tel: 9182 3202, admission fee, July and Aug daily; Apr, June–Sept daily except Fri and Sun; Jan–Mar and Oct–Dec Mon–Thurs) features a reconstructed front-line trench from the 1916 World War I battle, on the first day of which more than 2,000 Ulster volunteer soldiers died.

Overlooking the town is **Scrabo Tower** (Scrabo Country Park, tel: 9181 1491, hours vary), a 19th-century memorial to the third Marquess of Londonderry, offering splendid vistas of the lough and the soft-hilled countryside and good walks in the nearby **Killynether Wood**.

★**Donaghadee ㊳**, 13 km (8 miles) to the east, is notable for its much-painted harbour and lighthouse, and summer boat trips (Nelson's Boats, 07811 230215) up Belfast Lough and to **Copeland Island** (a bird sanctuary), just offshore. The twisting road passes the 18th-century **Ballycopeland Windmill** (Millisle, 9054 6552, Tues–Sat & Sun pm, Jul–Aug) and quieter beaches at **Ballywalter** and **Ballyhalbert**, and the fishing port of **Portavogie**, which has occasional evening quayside fish auctions.

BANGOR

Bangor ㊴ was orginally a small seaside resort, noted for its abbey. The expensively rejuvenated seafront still has to gentrify some of its collection of fast-food bars and souvenir shops to do justice to the spanking new marina packed with yachts and cruisers. Rowing around the bay in hired punts and fishing trips from the pier are evergreen attractions. The town has a leisure centre with heated swimming and diving pools. For some reason, perhaps the bracing sea air, Bangor is favoured by evangelists who trawl for souls along the sea wall by the little harbour.

The **North Down Heritage Centre** (Castle Park Avenue, tel: 9127 1200, closed Sunday am, Mon except public holidays) showcases 2,500-year-old swords, a 9th-century handbell and 400-year-old maps.

The old Bangor has been overgrown by acres of new housing developments and shopping centres, many of them inhabited by people who work in Belfast. It is a

busy shopping town with a weekly open-air market, plenty of pubs and eating places, and parkland. The best beach is nearby **Ballyholme Bay**, a sandy arc which becomes very crowded when the sun shines.

If you leave Bangor by the A2, a signposted detour to the right will take in the beaches of **Helen's Bay**, the nearby wooded **Crawfordsburn Country Park** (tel: 028: 9185 3621, free), and the picturesque village of ★**Crawfordsburn** with its charming **Old Inn** *(see restaurant and hotel listings on pages 116 and 127)*. Such havens are unusual so close to a city the size of Belfast.

THE "GOLD COAST"

The A2 from Bangor to Belfast runs through what locals enviously describe as the **"Gold Coast"**. This is stockbroker country, where lush lawns meet mature woodland. Hillside sites, overlooking the shipping lanes, have traditionally lured the well-heeled.

Cultra, 10 km (6 miles) from Bangor, has leafy lanes, splendid houses, and the resplendent **Culloden Hotel** *(see page 126)*. They go in for yachting, golf and horse riding around here. Nowhere is more removed from the TV image of Northern Ireland.

Holywood, an ancient religious settlement a mile further on, enjoys a quiet prosperity since it was bypassed. Nothing much happens here, apart from summer jazz and rumours of the odd dance around the Maypole (supposedly the only one in Ireland), but it has pleasant shops, and good pubs and restaurants.

Nearby, at Cultra Manor is the **Ulster Folk and Transport Museum** ⑳ *(see pages 78 and 120)*.

Holy Bangor
A monastery founded in Bangor by St Comgall in the 6th century attracted thousands of students and teachers from all over Europe and was the starting point for missionaries as they in turn set off in their flimsy coracles to spread God's word throughout Europe. But the monastery was destroyed in a devastating Viking raid in AD 824 in which 3,000 people died.

Below: the Old Inn at Crawfordsburn
Bottom: traditional fun at Bangor's Pickie Pool

Cultural Influences

ARCHITECTURE

His insane wife committed, the novelist William Makepeace Thackeray came to Ireland, full of pathos, characterising Belfast in his 1843 *Irish Sketch-Book* as 'hearty, thriving and prosperous, as if it had money in its pockets and roast beef for dinner'. Another Englishman had arrived a few years earlier and already had his feet tucked under those moneyed tables. He was Charles Lanyon, architect, carpet-bagger and engineer. He came to Belfast from a then less prosperous Dublin, where he gained preference by marrying the boss's daughter, and was to change the city's architectural language for ever.

Lanyon's legacy

He put his signature to the Antrim Coast Road, to railway viaducts and to The Frosses, avenues of firs planted to secure the bog roads. Designing Georgian country houses gained access to the milieu he sought. He conferred on new bank buildings the majestic solidity of the *palazzi* of northern Italian merchant princes. He understood the essence of the architectural faddishness. He caught the spirit of early Victorian righteousness.

His Piranesian Crumlin Road County Gaol promises unbridled retribution. The County Courthouse's Corinthian exterior impresses with its lofty indifference, its courtrooms with academic disdain. Queen's University's spoof Elisabethanry appropriates unashamedly Oxford's Magdalen. His Doric facade of the Union Theological College promises dour Presbyterianism. His Palladian Custom House intimidates. And among his 14 churches, the campanile of Sinclair Seamen's stands as a beacon for night-time sailors.

Fall from grace

While Lanyon was knighted, became the city's mayor and one of its Conservative MPs, he was tainted with scandal. He was a known philanderer, and openly bought election votes. An unscrupulous property speculator, he shamelessly rigged public architectural competitions to his favour, and to the disadvantage of his great rival, W. J. Barre. However, Barre had the last laugh. A public outcry forced the City to award Barre, not Lanyon, the contract to design a memorial to Queen Victoria's Consort, Prince Albert. This loss, to a man so conscious of status, was a bitter blow.

Opposite: the grandeur of Parliament Buildings
Below: Charles Lanyon, who made his mark on Belfast
Bottom: his Union Theological College, dating from 1853

ART AS HISTORY, ART AS MURAL

The sectarian divide between Protestant and Catholic has long been an artistic preoccupation in Belfast. A century after Protestant William of Orange defeated his Catholic father-in-law James II at the 1690 Battle of the Boyne, artisan coach painters celebrated with gable-end paintings of 'King Billy' riding triumphant on his white horse. When partition in 1920 hived off Northern Ireland, triumphalist Orange murals were encouraged, deflecting the attention of poor Protestants from chronic unemployment and miserable housing.

A changing message

Until the 1981 IRA hunger strike, nationalists and republicans confined their icons inside political and sporting clubs. Then, with a growing confidence that they would triumph over Protestants as Protestants had over them, republican murals were born. Protestant murals, on the other hand, had been restricted to references to 1920s gun running, portraits of English Royals, biblical prophesies interpreted to their tradition, and portraits of William. Now Protestant paramilitaries saw their role as defenders of the faith. Contemporary military hardware appeared.

Along Sandy Row, the Shankill and the Newtownards Road, working-class Protestant heartlands, there are murals for the UDA (Ulster Defence Association), UDF (Ulster Defence Force), UVF (Ulster Volunteer Force), UFF (Ulster Freedom Fighters) and other loyalist organisations.

The UDA's murals hark back to the B-Specials (a loyalist paramilitary police force disbanded in 1969) and to Cuchulainn, Hound of Ulster, leader of the 100BC Red Branch Knights. He secured Ulster when he beat Scotland in a race to the shore by tossing his amputated hand ahead of him. Thus the Red Hand of Ulster, clenched, became the icon of some loyalist organisations.

Meanwhile, in Catholic north and west Belfast, the icons became the lily of the 1916 Easter Rising, Cuchulainn (on the republican side), dead hunger strikers and expressions of solidarity with Mexican and Basque revolutionaries. Some read '*saoirse*' (freedom). Others display a mordant wit in such altered traffic signs as 'sniper at work'.

Derry's walls

The other noted collection of murals is in the Bogside area of Derry City. Most famous is the 'Free Derry' mural declaring the area's 'independence' from British rule.

MEN WHO MARCH

Northern Ireland is unique in its flourishing popular culture: there are bands in every village and every housing estate. There are many processions throughout the year, and some quiet church parades, but the 'marching season' in July and August can heighten sectarian tensions.

The main Orange procession, which celebrates the 1690 Battle of the Boyne in which William III (William of Orange) cemented the Protestant heritage, takes place on 12 July. In Belfast, the main 12 July Orange parade is a massive affair that can take up to four hours to pass any given point. It attracts followers from all over the world.

On 13 July, the Black Men (the Orange Order's elite) dress up in period costume to re-enact King Billy's routing of the Catholic King James II in the "Sham Fight" at Scarva, County Down. On 12 August the Apprentice Boys march through Derry City in memory of 13 apprentices who closed the city's gates against the besieging forces of James II.

Lady's Day, in honour of the Madonna, Mary Mother of God, is held on 15 August by the Ancient Order of Hibernians, who are sometimes known as the Green Orangemen. (Green symbolises Catholic Ireland, orange Protestant Ulster.) Like their Orange counterparts, the Hibernians mix prayer with pageantry.

Before 1969, many hoped that such pageantry would become less political and more of a tourist attraction. Instead, many Catholics see it as "triumphalism" and many Protestants as another nationalist provocation.

Bands of hope
The world-famous flautist James Galway started his career in a Belfast band, and there can be few other parts of Europe where such a high percentage of the population plays a musical instrument. It's been calculated that, at a typical small-town piping contest in summer, you can hear £2.5 million worth of pipes keening away.

Below: an Ancient Order of Hibernians march, Derry City
Bottom: Orangemen on their 12 July parade in Belfast

Literary Lives

When the playwright Samuel Beckett complained of the pupils he taught at Belfast's prestigious Campbell College from 1927 to 1928, his headmaster asked whether he was aware that they were the cream of Ulster society. 'Yes, rich,' Beckett replied, 'and thick.'

Luckily, few writers have been so disparaging and the city no longer automatically doffs its literary cap to its sister capital south of the border. True, Swift but lusted for Jane Waring of Waring Street. True, Oscar Wilde did little but be educated at Portora, 160km (100 miles) west, and praise the city's architecture. True, James Joyce's connection is limited to questions he put in Paris to Maurice James Craig, inspiring Craig's poem *May the Lord in His Mercy Look Down on Belfast*. But the 1947 Education Act enabled many to send the first ever of their name to university. Thus many of the greatest poets writing today in the English language cite Belfast as their catalyst. Indeed, round the Queen's University campus, there are the makings of a resonating literary trail, awaiting an entrepreneur.

Below: novelist Brian Moore
Bottom: Maggie Smith and Bob Hoskins in the 1987 movie of his novel The Lonely Passion of Judith Hearne

Today's poets

The Nobel Laureate Seamus Heaney, who came from a Derry farming family, lived in Ashley Avenue and held workshops in a previous flat in Fitzwilliam Street. Many poets who passed through those critical sessions cite somewhere within a mile or so as their proving ground. Michael Longley writes of the Lisburn Road. Derek Mahon drank in Lavery's Gin Palace.

Tom Paulin grew up in Belfast. James Simmons edited *The Honest Ulsterman* literary magazine from Eglantine Avenue. Paul Muldoon was a Queen's man. Frank Ormsby immortalised King William Park, Ciarán Carson the Fly bar, Padaic Fiacc the Holy Land east of the campus where playwrights Bill Morrison and Stewart Parker shared a flat, later rented by the novelist Maurice Leitch.

Philip Larkin was assistant librarian at Queen's. The novelist and short-story writer Bernard McLaverty graduated from Queen's in 1974, his stories throwing light on the repressed Catholic sexualities of the early 1960s.

Yesterday's giants

Of an earlier generation, the prickly Ulster-Scots poet John Hewitt and E. M. Forster's friend, the novelist Forrest Reid, lived in Mount Charles. Part of poet Louis

MacNeice's childhood was spent in 77 Malone Road, a bishop's palace, now the Arts Council of NI's headquarters. C. S. Lewis was educated at Campbell College. The novelist Brian Moore (1921–99) spent his childhood in the shadow of King Billy's equestrian statue on Clifton Street, but he wrote perceptively of the suffocating narrow conventions and sexual repressions that wrought such gloom and distress among his class-conscious priest-ridden contemporaries in fine novels, including *The Lonely Passion of Judith Hearne*.

Below: C.S. Lewis, who grew up in east Belfast
Bottom: Nobel prizewinning poet Seamus Heaney

The short story writer Sam McAughtry mined a different seam, reinventing the narrow red-brick streets of his impoverished Protestant childhood. Robert Harbinson, born in 1928 as Robert Harbinson Bryans in evangelical working-class east Belfast, reworked his life as cabin-boy, missionary and minor London literary lion in a series of autobiographical novels. John Boyd, a socialist from a not dissimilar background, put on his polemical plays at the Lyric Theatre while he was its literary manager.

Contemporary issues

Recent terrorism has led to many careers in confessional publishing, but of today's prose writers most pertinent are the novelists Glenn Patterson and Robert McLiam Wilson who grew up in the east and west of the city. Graham Reid's TV scripts and Gary Mitchell's plays, particularly *In a Little World of Our Own* and *As the Beast Sleeps*, open a window on to loyalist violence, while Ronan Bennet's screenplays reveal a more romantic perspective on the IRA.

FOOD AND DRINK

Apart from early pioneers such as celebrity chef Paul Rankin, Michael Deane and Nick Price, it wasn't until the peace process kicked in that good food became consistently easy to find in Belfast. Even today, it's hard to find the quality or variety of ethnic cuisine that, say, Londoners are used to. But Belfast dining is improving rapidly and good, well-priced food is available throughout the city, not least in pubs and cafés.

Breakfast (the artery-hardening Ulster Fry plus wheaten and soda breads) is what Belfast is famous for, but, as you'll find at St George's Market, there is terrific fresh fish and seafood, grass-reared meats and creamy Irish cheeses (admittedly mostly from the Republic) to be had too.

Belfast Restaurants

Prices indicate the cost of a three-course evening meal for two with a bottle of house wine, but not coffee or service.

£££ (Expensive: £75-plus)

Aldens, 229 Upper Newtownards Rd, tel: 9065 0079. This bistro in unfashionable east Belfast draws diners from around the city to excellent food.

Cayenne, 7 Ascot House, Shaftsbury Square, tel: 9033 1532. Paul Rankin's flagship is still one of the best restaurants in town and a regular award winner.

James St South, 21 James St South, tel: 9043 4370. Elegant new restaurant near City Hall has won plaudits for its un-pretentious quality.

Nick's Warehouse, 35 Hill Street, tel: 9043 9690. Longstanding Cathedral Quarter favourite (with wine bar and annexe) doesn't date.

Restaurant Michael Deane's, 36-40 Howard Street, tel: 9033 1134. As near to

Opposite: the Crown Liquor Saloon

formal as Belfast gets, with classic Michelin star cooking from one of the stars of the Belfast scene. More informal, cheaper and still high-quality is Deane's Brasserie downstairs. He's also introduced a New York-style deli around the corner.

Roscoff Brasserie, 7-11 Linenhall Street, tel: 9031 1150. Paul Rankin's latest venture takes the name of his pioneering Belfast restaurant for excellent French-inspired food.

Shu, 253 Lisburn Road, tel: 9038 1655. This stylish restaurant in Belfast's designer label heartland has picked up a swathe of awards for imaginative fusion cooking.

Ta Tu Bar and Grill 701 Lisburn Road, tel: 9042 1000**.** This glamorous venue serves good Californian-style and contemporary Irish food. Fine drinks list too.

Tedfords, 5 Donegall Quay, tel: 9043 4000. A converted ship's chandlers on the waterfront, known for its excellent seafood and fish dishes. Basement bar.

££ (Moderate: £50-plus)

Apartment, 2 Donegall Square, tel: 9050 9777. All-day menu available at this trendy bar with views of City Hall.

Beatrice Kennedy, 44 University Road, tel: 9020 2290. Virtually next door to Queen's University, this award-winning bistro's Sunday lunch has become a Belfast institution.

Café Milano, 92–94 Lisburn Road, tel: 9068 9777. Fountains, colourful frescoes and a large menu of Italian favourites makes this a good place to stop before a Lisburn Road shopping expedition.

Grill Room and Bar, Ten Square Hotel, 10 Donegall Sq South, tel: 9024 1001. Simple but excellent food at fair prices has made this all-day venue very popular.

Potthouse Bar and Grill, 1 Hill Street, tel: 9024 4044. Modern Irish food served in stylish surroundings at Cathedral Quarter's latest and chicest venture.

Villa Italia, 37-41 University St, tel: 9032 8356. Expect to queue at this Queen's Quarter favourite for classic Italian food, Belfast-style. Family favourite.

Zen, 55–59 Adelaide Street, tel: 9023 2244. Enjoyable Japanese fusion cooking in a strikingly converted linen warehouse near City Hall.

£ (Moderate: £50-plus)

Café Renoir, 93–95 Botanic Avenue. tel: 9031 1300. Welcoming bistro/café with imaginative fare and superb wood-fired oven pizzas next door.

Flour Crepe Room, 46 Upper Queen Street, tel: 9033 9966. Large range of sweet and savoury crepes served to order. Anything from smoked salmon and cream cheese to Bailey's Irish Cream.

John Hewitt Bar and Restaurant, 51 Donegall Street, tel: 9023 3768. Atmospheric pub in Cathedral Quarter offers modern Irish comfort food and Asian-influenced cuisine. Good desserts.

McHughs, 29–31 Queen's Square, tel: 9050 9990. Wok cooking or traditional Irish stews and champ at this restored pub in Belfast's oldest waterfront building.

Northern Whig, 2 Bridge Street, tel: 9050 9888. Popular Soviet-themed pub; versatile all-day menu.

Sun Kee, 43–47 Donegall Pass. tel: 9031, 2016. Unlike the average Belfast Chinese,

Fresh seafood is excellent but pricey

this doesn't cater solely for local tastes.

Tao, 79 Dublin Road, tel: 9032 7788. You can find virtually every kind of Chinese noodle dish available as well as a massive TV screen at this funky noodle bar.

Restaurants outside Belfast

Dinner for two with bottle of house wine but not coffee or service:

    £££ = expensive (£75-plus)
    ££ = moderate (£50-plus)
    £ = inexpensive (under £50)

ANTRIM COAST ROAD

Bushmills Inn, Dunluce Road, Bushmills. Co Antrim, tel: 2073 2339. Popular hotel with reputation for fine food. Near Bushmills distillery. **££**

Londonderry Arms Hotel, 20 Harbour Rd, Carnlough, Co Antrim, tel: 2888 5255. Charming hotel in fishing village serving good, traditional style food. **££**

The Thatch Inn, 57 Main Street, Broughshane, Ballymena, tel: 2586 1366. Multi-award winning traditional pub with wide range of good and inexpensive food. **£**

The Watermargin, Coleraine. Boat-house, Hanover Place, Coleraine, Co Antrim, tel: 7034 2222. From Chinese Irish-style to the real thing. Busy. **£**

The Wine Bar and Harbour Bistro, Portrush Harbour, Co Antrim, tel: 7082 4313. Good, reasonably priced food for all the family. **£**

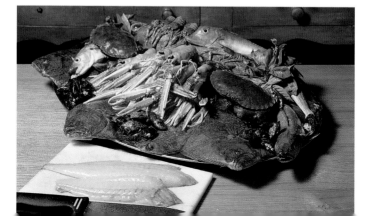

DERRY

Beech Hill Country House. 32 Ardmore Road, Derry, tel: 7134 9279. Luxurious hotel in spacious grounds with gourmet dining, 2 miles (3 km) from Derry City's walls. **£££**

Browns Brasserie, 1 Bonds Hill, Waterside, Derry, tel: 7134 5180. Popular and atmospheric Waterside brasserie with inventive and reliable food. **££**

Fiorentini's, 67 Strand Terrace, Derry, tel: 7126 0653. Good stop for families, with Italian ice cream and choice of child-friendly food. **£**

Fitzroys, 2–4 Bridge Street, tel: 7126 6211. Welcoming city-centre bistro with strong Mediterranean influences. Open all day. **££**

La Sosta Ristorante, 45a Carlisle Road, tel: 7137 4817. Family-run Italian eatery five minutes' walk from city centre. **£**

The Lime Tree, Catherine Street, Limavady. tel: 7776 4300. Family-run restaurant which uses locally sourced seafood to great effect. **££**

DONEGAL

Kealys Seafood Bar, Harbour, Greencastle, Co. Donegal, tel: (00 353) 74 938 1010. The freshest seafood and fish, simply but perfectly cooked. **£**

The Mill, Figart, Dunfanaghy, tel: (00 353) 74 913 6985. A wonderfully relaxing place to stay and eat on the shores of the New Lake, with beautifully cooked food eaten by an open fire. **££**

Rathmullan House, Rathmullan, Co Donegal, tel: (00 353) 74 915 8188. Gracious living and fine dining at lovely country house hotel on shores of Lough Swilly. **£££**

CO TYRONE

Ardbeg Lodge, 32 Dungannon Road, Ballygawley, tel: 8556 8517. Good, reliable country comfort cooking with no pretensions. **££**

Otter Lodge, 26 Dungannon Road, Cookstown, tel: 8676 5427. Excellent

value at this bistro and wine bar in a pretty riverbank setting. **£**

Stangmore Town House, 24 Killymain Road, Dungannon, tel: 8772 5600. Lovely gardens at this Georgian-style guest-house with excellent food available to non-residents. **£££**

FERMANAGH

Café Merlot/Restaurant 6, 6 Church Street, Enniskillen, tel: 6632 0918. Adjoining the famous Blakes of the Hollow pub, the acclaimed Café Merlot is modern Irish and Restaurant 6 offers fine dining. **££**

Francos Restaurant, Queen Elizabeth Road, Enniskillen, Co Fermanagh, tel: 6632 4183. Seafood, pizzas and pasta in informal setting. **£**

The Sheelin Restaurant, Main Street, Bellanaleck, tel: 6634 8232. Charming thatched cottage restaurant with superb cooking and fine wine list. **££**

The Thatch, Belleek, Co Fermanagh, tel: 6865 8181. Good traditional-style food at this coffee shop in a listed 18th-century building. Near Belleek China factory. **£**

ARMAGH

Basement Café, Market Street, Armagh, tel: 3752 4311. Good traditional Irish food alongside usual kids' fare make this city-centre café attractive for families. **£**

Manor Park Restaurant, 2 College Hill, The Mall, Armagh, tel: 3751 5353. Atmospheric French restaurant in a beautiful 19th-century building next to the Observatory. **££**

Market Place Theatre Restaurant, Market Place, Armagh, tel: 3752 1828. Fine bistro-style food, coffees and bar in this state-of-the-art theatre complex. Check for opening times. **£**

The Yellow Door, Woodhouse Street, Portadown, tel: 3835 3528. Award-winning restaurant and deli. **£**

Zio, 7 Market St, Armagh, tel: 3752 2299. Friendly, atmospheric Italian with inviting pastas and pizzas. **£**

COUNTY DOWN AND THE MOURNES

Bucks Head, 77 Main Street, Dundrum, Co Down, tel: 4375 1868. One of Northern Ireland's finest gastro pubs, serving marvellous local seafood and fish. **££**

Canal Court, Merchants Quay, Newry, Co Down, tel: 3025 1234. Newry's award-winning hotel also serves good value family meals. **££**

Duke Restaurant, Duke Street, Warrenpoint, Co Down, tel: 4175 2084. Surprisingly good seafood, fish and steaks above pub. **££**

Mourne Seafood Bar, 10 Main Street, Dundrum, tel: 4375 1377. A highly acclaimed restaurant specialising in locally caught fish and seafood. **£**

The Plough, the Square, Hillsborough, Co. Down, tel: 9268 2985. Usually packed family-run pub in lovely Georgian village. One of Northern Ireland's best gastro pubs, serving substantial portions of inventive food. **££**

ARDS PENINSULA

The Old Inn, Crawfordsburn, Co. Down, tel: 9185 3255. Atmospheric and unspoilt old inn which was a favourite of C.S. Lewis and, allegedly, entertained Peter the Great. Its **Restaurant 1614** takes its award-winning food very seriously. **£££**

Portaferry Hotel, the Strand, Portaferry, Co Down, tel: 4272 8231. Long cherished hotel and restaurant on shores of beautiful Strangford Lough. **££**

Villa Toscana, Toscana Park West Circular Road, Bangor, tel: 9147 3737. Good, inexpensive, child-friendly palatial Italian restaurant. **£**

Pick of Belfast's pubs

The *Concise Ulster Dictionary* says *crack* (drink, badinage, music) derives from the Ulster Scots tongue, not the Gaelic *craic* as you might expect. Even so, this peculiarly Irish term has always been far more associated with Dublin than Belfast. It's taken a long time to break down this misconception, but the signs are that more and more visitors are coming to Belfast precisely for its growing reputation as a party town.

For anyone wandering the often thinly populated streets of the city centre after office hours this might seem a dubious claim, but spend an evening in good company in a good Belfast pub and you'll find the reputation for friendliness and humour is largely deserved. Head on to the growing number of energetic dance clubs, and you can enjoy a genuine party atmosphere, free of the pretentiousness and aloofness of rival cities.

If you have the time, the easiest way to explore the best of the old-fashioned Belfast pubs in the city-centre is on a **Historical Pubs Tour** (tel: 9268 3665 or visit www.belfastpubtours.com, May to October inc), which leaves from the Crown Dining Rooms, above the **Crown Liquor Saloon** on Great Victoria Street, each Thursday at 7pm and Saturday at 4pm. The tours usually last two hours, with a chance to sample six of a changing roster of nine or ten different pubs.

Beneath the **Crown Dining Rooms** is Belfast's most famous pub, the **Crown Liquor Saloon** (Great Victoria St, tel: 9027 9901). It may be more self-conscious of its tourist appeal these days, but don't ignore its delightful craftsmanship – exquisite tile and glass work – and atmospheric snugs.

The Duke of York (7 Commercial Court, tel: 9024 1062) is a former journalists' pub (though most famous for former barman Gerry Adams), hence the printing artefacts, and retains an old fashioned intimacy. It offers a pretty good mix of live music and disco too.

Bittles Bar (103 Victoria St, tel: 9031 1088) is a distinctive triangular pub with a literary feel. It was once known as The Shakespeare, and you'll encounter a large assortment of Ireland's literary giants, from Wilde to Joyce, on the walls of its tri-cornered lounge.

The Garrick (29 Chichester Street, tel: 9033 3875) is a nicely restored old lawyers' pub, with gaslights outside and beautiful tiled floors inside.

So old (established in 1720) that it was once a country pub, **Kelly's Cellars** has attracted a fair share of bohemians and revolutionaries in its time and still has an interesting mix of clientele.

Another ancient pub – though, like Kelly's, the decor is traditional-like but not original – **White's Tavern** (2–4 Winecellar Entry, tel: 9023 6232) can be found down a cobble-stoned entry. Interesting artefacts around the pub and a pleasant atmosphere. Music, including good folk sessions, upstairs at weekends.

The most genuinely Irish bar in town is **Madden's** (74 Berry St, tel: 9024 4114), where the sound of fiddle playing beckons you into the small friendly pub most nights.

McHugh's (29-31 Queen's Square, tel: 9050 9990), in what is claimed to be Belfast's oldest building, has been skilfully renovated with exposed original brickwork and beams and a ship's boiler built into the walls. It has regular live music and a restaurant serving Asian or traditional Irish grub.

Grub of an altogether kind can be found at the listed **Morning Star** (17–19 Pottinger's Entry, tel: 9032 3976), a former coaching house and old-fashioned pub whose Australian co-owner is liable to include emu or kangaroo or even crocodile on the menu.

Claiming to have utilised the talents of some of the craftsmen who worked on the *Titanic*, **Hatfield House** (130 Ormeau Rd, tel: 9043 8764) is an attractive pub, despite its large screens for sport, with a lively roster of music and entertainment.

John Hewitt was a famous, and influential Belfast poet. The Cathedral Quarter pub named after him (51 Donegall St, tel: 9023 3768) has a strong cultural flavour, with literary events and a regular line-up of Irish and jazz music. Though of recent origin, this community-run pub, with award-winning food, feels more traditional than many far older rivals. It is a major venue during the Cathedral Quarter Arts Festival.

For many, **the Kitchen Bar** (now 36–40 Victoria Square, tel: 9032 4901) was the most genuine of Belfast's traditional pubs. Forced to move to an old Victorian seed warehouse around the corner after its old home was demolished to make way for the Victoria Square retail development, the atmosphere has changed from quirky intimacy to spacious elegance. All the same, it's still friendly, still serves, unusually for Belfast, an interesting choice of beers, offers live traditional Irish and jazz music, and the food offering is still based on fine home

The spacious Kitchen Bar

cooking and remains excellent value (the Paddy's Pizza – pizza ingredients on soda bread – is a favourite).

Even the Kitchen Bar can't compete with the **Rotterdam** (54 Pilot St, 9074 6021) in Sailortown, for live music. Blues, rock, folk or jazz, the bar has long been famous as the home of pub music in Belfast. In summer, there's alfresco music in adjacent Barrow Square.

Around the corner is another appealing pub with excellent traditional music, **Pat's Bar** (19 Princes Dock St. tel: 9074 4524), which shares Barrow Square for outdoor music events.

Speaking of alfresco, for long summer evenings, it would be hard to beat sitting outside **Cutter's Wharf** (Lockview Rd, Stranmillis, tel: 9080 5100), on the banks of the Lagan, watching boats and swans drift by. The recently refurbished bar and restaurant are popular.

Another pub with an outdoor drinking area is the **Kings Head** (829 Lisburn Rd, tel: 9050 9950) with a popular beer garden in which you can enjoy their bar menu, jazz brunches on Sunday and barbecue nights on summer Sundays. Their Live Lounge has music and comedy and there's a large restaurant too.

Nightlife

Belfast has earned a surprising reputation for a new generation of stylish bars and nightclubs. Perhaps hedging its bets, the **Robinson's** complex, next to the Crown, includes the now rather dated-looking but still popular Irish-themed pub, Fibber Magee's, but also the quirkily upmarket BT1 and even newer Roxy, home to dance nights and live music.

Another big draw is the eastern-influenced **Bar Bacca** (43 Franklin St, tel: 9023 0200) a 'Best Bar in all-Ireland' winner in 2002, with a large and inventive range of cocktails and regular DJ's. Upstairs is sister nightclub **La Lea**.

Another cocktail menu worth inves-

tigating is at the kitsch US-style 1950s interior of the popular **Irene and Nan's**.

Huge jars of cocktails and a regular party atmosphere help make **The Fly** (5-6 Lower Crescent Road, tel: 9050 9750) a honeypot for students.

Another of the original style bars that Belfast took to its heart is the **Northern Whig** (2 Bridge St, tel: 9050 9888), housed in what was once an old Belfast newspaper office. Now Soviet-themed (big chunky furniture, several vodka-based cocktails, statues of Lenin etc), its bar, restaurant and nightclub are usually heaving on weekends.

Milk attracts large queues to the unpromising Tomb St to nights of r&b, funk, soul, hip-hop and house as well as various party themes.

In the Queen's Quarter, **the M-Club** in Bradbury Place and **Shine**, run by Queen's University Student Union, are renowned as major dance venues.

The **Potthouse** (1 Hill St, tel: 9024 4044), in the Cathedral Quarter drink-and-dance scene, has a bar and grill downstairs and Sugar Room nightclub upstairs.

The Gay Scene

Fundamentalist Protestants still condemn homosexuals to the fires of hell, but the gay scene is more relaxed than it used to be, particularly in Belfast. Here, it is centred on the Cathedral Quarter, where the Union St Bar and Restaurant (8–14 Union St, tel: 9031 6060) and sister nightclub, the Kremlin (96 Donegall St, tel: 9031 6060) are adjoining. The Nest, (tel: 9024 5558) recently refurbished, is at 22–28 Skipper Street and Mynt (2–16 Dunbar Street, tel: 9023 4520) is on the outer reaches of the area. Gay-friendly pubs include Apartment (2 Donegall Square) and John Hewitt (51 Donegall St).

● Northern Ireland Gay Rights Association (tel: 9066 4111) holds meeetings at Cathedral Buildings, 64 Donegall St.

● www.belfastpride.com has details of early August's Gay Pride Week (parade, disco evenings, etc).

● www.gaybelfast.net covers events for visitors.

TOURS

There are various ways to explore Belfast, from the black taxi tours to cycling, bus, coach, boat and walking tours.

Much of Belfast's history is contained in the fairly small and accessible city-centre, which forms the basis of **Walking Tours of Belfast**'s Historical Tours. Using specially trained Blue Badge guides, these 90-minute tours take place from May to October and, like most of the other tours, can be booked at the **Belfast Welcome Centre**, 47 Donegall Place (tel: 9024 6609).

The many different **Black Taxi** guides do not need the Blue Badge accreditation and the commentary is entirely subjective, and no less enjoyable for that. But the advantage here, apart from the relief to your feet, is you can personalise your tour, whether you want to head for the political murals or the home of *Titanic*. One of these is Ken Harper (tel: 9074 2711, Mob: 0771 1757 178) who also customises tours to explore the origins of the three famous sons of east Belfast, C.S. Lewis, Van Morrison and George Best.

Belfast by Bike (available at the Belfast Welcome Centre) informs you of the National Cycle Network lanes around the city. You can hire a bike at McConvey's Cycles (183 Ormeau Road, tel: 028 9033 0322), just yards away from one of these routes, and spend a delightful day cycling up the Lagan towpath and back, perhaps taking a picnic to the famous Rose Garden at Sir Thomas and Lady Dixon Park.

The lure of *Titanic* proves a bigger draw each year to Belfast. The **Lagan Boat Company** has regular boat trips to the Harland and Wolff shipyards where she was built and you can see the drawing rooms where she was designed, her dry dock, the slipway from which she was launched and even the steam cranes that lowered her down. They also have boat trips down the Lagan river. Call the Belfast Welcome Centre for booking or visit the www.laganboatcompany.com website for more information.

You can tour the city on an open-topped bus with **Belfast City Sightseeing** (tel: 9062 6888). The tour includes the Botanic Gardens, the Harland and Wolf shipyards and the famous wall murals of the Falls and Shankill. They also run a Stormont tour which includes the Harland and Wolf shipyards as well as the Northern Ireland parliament buildings. **Mini-Coach** (tel: 9031 5333) also include the Titanic Quarter as part of their Belfast City Tour.

You can meet local people and trace your links with the United Irishmen, *Titanic* or George Best with the unique **Belfast Safaris** tours (c/o Spectrum Centre, 331 Shankill Road, tel: 9022 2925). Enthralling **Belfast Literary Tours** leave the Linen Hall Library each Mon (March to Oct), tel: 9024 6609 for details.

Finally, **Coiste** (10 Beechmount Ave, tel: 9020 0770), a republican ex-prisoners group have daily political tours of west Belfast, starting at the Divis Tower. Given time, and if you have a large group to keep costs down, they can customise a detailed political tour, meeting with politicians and campaign groups and handing you over to a loyalist tour guide at the peace wall.

Black taxis provide city tours

BELFAST FOR FAMILIES

The **Odyssey complex** (tel: 9046 7030), on Belfast's waterfront, is a good place to keep children amused on rainy days. With several attractions to choose from, it's not hard to spend a good day or two in its environs, with numerous cafés and restaurants to keep the energy levels up. Most impressive of its offerings is W5, "an interactive discovery centre". Over several floors, 140 exhibits encourage kids to take part in all kinds of entertaining activities, without being aware of the scientific principles they are absorbing. There's also a 20-lane tenpin bowling alley; huge IMAX cinema and a 12-screen cinema complex.

The Belfast Giants ice hockey team have the adjoining **Odyssey Arena** as their home base and following them has become a local family sport.

Other indoor attractions include the **Ulster Museum** (Botanic Gardens, tel: 9038 3000) which has exhibitions of Irish history, archaeology and a 'Made in Belfast' exhibit. Child-friendly, it also has a nature programme, excellent collection of Irish and British art and much else. The museum will re-open in 2009 after an extensive £12.5 million facelift and extension.

Ulster Folk and Transport Museum

An Olympic-sized ice rink and ten-pin bowling with lanes and bowls that light up, as well as a kids' adventure playground, is on offer at **Dundonald International Ice Bowl** (111 Old Dundonald Rd, tel: 028 9080 9100) in east Belfast.

Next door, the **Pirates Adventure Golf** (tel: 9048 0220) has two courses, one covered, for putting on greens. Pirate schooners provide atmosphere.

Nearby, **Streamvale Open Farm** (38 Ballyhandwood Rd, tel: 9048 3244) is open from Easter to the end of August, and has various baby domestic animals, tractor rides and wildlife walks.

Aunt Sandra's Candy Factory (60 Castlereagh Rd, tel: 9073 2868), allows children to watch confectionery being made as it was traditionally in this area until the 1950s.

In decent weather, one essential visit for any family is the award-winning **Ulster Folk and Transport Museum**, where a 1900s town of original Ulster buildings has been recreated, with traditional skills such as blacksmiths and weavers, being demonstrated. It also has a splendid transport section, *Titanic* exhibition, miniature railway (in summer) and the X2 Flight Experience, which incorporates interactive science exhibits, historic aircraft and eight-seater flight simulator. Exhibits range from horse-drawn chariots right up to a prototype of the ill-fated Belfast-built De Lorean sports car (star of the *Back to the Future* movies). The museum is just outside the city in Cultra *(see page 78)*, but barely a 30-minute ride from the city centre on Bangor-bound trains or buses.

A little nearer is **Belfast Zoo** (tel: 9077 6277) high up in Cave Hill at the edges of North Belfast, which has won awards for its conservation programmes with rare animals and has a programme of special events. Some unusual animals, such as Malaysian tapirs, have been born here.

DIARY OF ANNUAL EVENTS

JANUARY

Early January: End of Christmas pantos at Grand Opera House, Waterfront Hall and Lyric Theatre.

January: Drama, music, literary events, comedy and more at the Out To Lunch Festival, organised by the Cathedral Quarter Arts Festival.

March 17: St Patrick's Day celebrations for Ireland's national saint. (See also Downpatrick details on page 100.)

April: Titanic Made in Belfast festival at venues round city, including Harland and Wolff shipyards. World Irish Dancing Championships (2006). Belfast Film Festival, a series of masterclasses, premieres and talks.

April/May: Cathedral Quarter Arts Festival, highly rated contemporary arts festival in Belfast's cultural sector.

May: Belfast Children's Festival, an imaginative series of events run by Young at Art at venues around city, including the Botanic Gardens.

Mid-May: Northern Ireland's premier agricultural show at King's Hall.

May 1: Belfast Marathon.

May: Lord Mayor's Show. Parade and festivities around city-centre.

Early June: Holywood pub Jazz Festival, 10 miles east of Belfast.

Mid-June: Castleward Opera season in grounds of stately home on shores of Strangford Lough, 30 miles (50 km) southeast of the city.

Early July: The Ulster Senior Hurling Finals, Casement Park.

11 July: Bonfire Night

12 July: Belfast 'Twelfth' parade with marching bands and bowler hats. Recent 'family-friendly' innovations have included King Billy handing out confectionery to watching children. The main celebration is at 'the field' (usually a Belfast park) afterwards.

Mid-July: World-famous International Rose Trials at Sir Thomas and Lady Dixon

Park (Upper Malone Road, south Belfast).

July: Opera in the Gardens. Live link-up to London's Royal Opera House from Botanic Gardens.

July/August: Belfast Pride, six-day festival for Belfast's gay and lesbian community.

Early August: Féile an Phobail, a celebration of republican culture, with drama, comedy, music of all kinds and much else throughout west Belfast.

15 August: West Belfast's Ancient Order of Hibernians parade, akin to the Orangemen's Twelfth, only smaller.

August: Tennent's Vital Festival. Top rock acts over two days in the Botanic Gardens.

Late August: Ulster Grand Prix, the on-road motorcycle classic, at Dundrod, near International Airport. Belfast Mela, the Indian communities' increasingly popular celebration in the Botanic Gardens.

September: Proms in the Park, live music and live-link up to Last Night at the Proms outside City Hall.

September: Garden Gourmet weekend in Botanic Gardens, a festival of food and flowers.

October: Open House traditional music festival, usually as part of Queen's fest (see below)

31 October: Hallowe'en ghosts and ghouls at various waterfront venues, including spectacular fireworks.

October/November: Belfast Festival at Queen's, Ireland's finest, a three-week gourmandising of concert, gig, drama and exhibition taking on something of the spirit of the Edinburgh Festival.

Early December: Cinemagic International Film Festival for the young. C.S. Lewis Festival, celebrating the Belfast-born creator of Narnia. Christmas Lights Switch-On and Christmas Markets, City Hall. Lamplight Procession from St Anne's Cathedral.

SHOPPING

Until the arrival of the peace process, Belfast wasn't the most relaxing place to shop. The army patrolled the streets, security guards frisked you as you entered the major stores and people tended to get their heads down and target just what they needed. Today, it's a different story. All the big names from the British High Street can be found around the city centre and large shopping centres like **Castle-Court,** on Royal Avenue (70 stores ranging from **Debenhams** to **Virgin**) will soon be dwarfed by the Victoria Square retail development. The area around Royal Avenue and Donegall Pass represents the hub of Belfast shopping but other parts of the city have their own appeal.

Followers of fashion can discover virtually every designer label they want somewhere in the city centre or along the Lisburn Road. High men's fashion, from Paul Smith to Gieves, can be found at the spacious **Bureau** at 46–50 Howard Street (tel: 9032 6100), while a more street-fashion approach is shown by their sister shop, **Grand Magasin** (1–4 Wellington St, tel: 9043 9800).

On the other side of City Hall, the Georgian townhouse belonging to top local designer **Michelle O'Doherty** (7–9 Chichester Street, 028-9023 3303), houses some of fashion's most illustrious names and her own ready to wear collection. The long-established **Fresh Garbage** at 24 Rosemary St (tel: 9024 23, is for the alternative (Goth, hippy, punk etc) fashion collector while retro US clothes and much else can also be found nearby at **Liberty Blue** (19–21 Lombard Street, tel: 9043 7745).

The success of its linen industry made a huge contribution to the development of Belfast. Today, you can still find locally-made linen products, including made to measure tableware, at **Smyth's Irish Linens** (tel: 9024 2232) at 55–59 Royal Avenue. Beautifully tailored hand-finished Irish linen shirts are among the main attractions at the very upmarket **Smyth and Gibson** (tel: 9023 0388) at Bedford House, Bedford Street.

In the same location is **Steensons** (tel: 9024 8269), where Bill and Christina Steenson's contemporary Irish jewellery has proved a long-standing success. **Queen's Arcade**, off Donegall Place, is also a centre for jewellery shops.

Best of the Irish crafts shops is the **Wicker Man** at 12 Donegall Arcade (tel: 9024 3550) with a large range of Irish knitwear, Celtic jewellery, hand thrown Irish pottery and much more. **Utopia** in the Fountains Centre, College St (tel: 9024 1342) has distinctive gifts from around the world like stylish Italian chess sets and traditional handmade Russian lacquer boxes. **Open Window Productions** (tel: 9032 9669) at 25 Donegall Street has specially created chess sets of the peace process, Middle East (Osama v Bush), and the *Titanic*.

Smithfield Market, at the junction of Winetavern and West Streets, can't compare with its much missed Victorian-built predecessor but still has some interesting shops to explore, from collectable models to comics.

For food, **Sawers** (tel: 9032 2021) at 7b Fountain Centre on College Street, is hard to beat for seafood delicacies, Irish smoked salmon and gourmet foods from around the world. **St George's Market** (Friday 6am–2pm Variety, and Saturday 10am–4pm City Food and Garden) has wonderful fish and seafood, organic meat and vegetables, Irish cheeses, speciality breads and much more.

Bradbury's art gallery and shop (2–3 Lyndon Court, Queen Street, tel: 9023 3535) is worth investigating and there are excellent fine art galleries along the Lisburn Road, with interesting antique shops on the otherwise unpromising Donegall Pass.

SPORT

GOLF

One of Belfast's most appealing attributes is its sense of openness and space. Nowhere is far from mountain, park, or that contemporary version of the countryside, the golf course. Northern Ireland regularly hits the top 10 in the world's top golfing destinations and Belfast certainly contributes to that exalted status.

Golfers will discover more than a dozen good courses, most within easy reach of the city centre. The daddy of them all is **Royal Belfast** (tel: 9042 8165), the oldest club in Ireland. Not always the easiest to visit (though staying at the adjacent Culloden hotel earns you special access), it has magnificent views of Belfast Lough and a challenging course that attracts leading golfers.

Literally minutes from the city centre, **Balmoral Golf Club** (tel: 9038 1514) is nearly as venerable as Royal Belfast and more easily accessible. A 2,276-yard parkland course, it was here that champion Irish golfer Fred Daly learnt the ropes. Good clubhouse, too.

Further out, in Carryduff, **Rockmount Golf Club** (tel: 9081 2279) has 120 acres of top-class golf, while **Belvoir** (tel: 9049 1693), which has hosted Irish opens, was judged by Gary Player one of the world's best parkland courses. It's also one of the most beautiful.

A good introduction to golf here is the **Belfast Golf Challenge**, which takes place at three of the most inviting courses in the city, Shandon Park, Dunmurry and Malone, each September and is open to all. Organised by Belfast City Council, you can find more details by visiting www.belfastcity.gov.uk/golfchallenge.

ICE HOCKEY

It's a slightly surreal concept but a recent sporting success story in Belfast has been the Belfast Giants ice hockey team who play at the Odyssey Arena (tel: 9073 9074). The 28 home games per season (Sept to April), are attended by capacity crowds of over 4,000.

BALL GAMES

Other top spectator sports include rugby, with the Ulster team playing regular Magners League and Heineken Cup fixtures at their Ravenhill headquarters (tel: 9049 3222) and soccer. Before leaving, Lawrie Sanchez rejuvenated the Northern Ireland side, which plays, as do Linfield FC, at Windsor Park ((tel: 9024 4198). Other Belfast Irish League soccer clubs include Glentoran, Crusaders and Cliftonville. For more information, contact the Irish Football Association (9066 9458; www.irishfa.com).

The GAA sports of hurling and football, can be enjoyed at Casement Park (tel: 9060 5868) in west Belfast.

ATHLETICS

International athletics meetings are held at the Mary Peters Track, named after the Northern Irish Olympic gold medallist, in Malone playing fields (for athletics enquiries, tel: 9060 2707).

The **Belfast Marathon** each May is a 24-mile (39-km) trot around the city (www.belfastcitymarathon.com).

HORSE RACING

The historic Down Royal racecourse (tel: 9262 1256), 10 miles (16 km) south of Belfast City centre, has a series of popular meetings through the year, including St Patrick's Day and the Northern Ireland Festival of Racing.

CYCLING

Lagan Towpath route takes cyclists past some lovely parks and the odd decent pub. For bike hire, McConvey's Cycles (tel: 9033 0322) is just yards away from the National Cycle Network lanes that begin this route.

PRACTICAL INFORMATION

Getting There

BY AIR

Belfast International (tel: 9448 4848), 19 miles (30 km) northwest of the city, is Northern Ireland's busiest airport with connections to the rest of the UK, Europe and the US. George Best Airport, formerly Belfast City Airport (tel: 9093 9093) is 3 miles (5 km) from the city centre.

Numerous daily services link **Belfast International** with Heathrow or Stansted (one hour) and many other UK airports. The main operator from here is Easyjet (www.easyjet.com) which flies to numerous European destinations. Other airlines include bmi baby (tel: 0870 264 2229), Continental (tel: 0845 607 6760) which flies to New York/ Newark, Jet2 (tel: 0871 226 1737) which flies to Barcelona, Prague and Leeds, and Wizz Air (tel: +48-22 351 9499) which flies to Katowice and Warsaw.

Belfast's George Best Airport has flights to several UK provincial airports, plus London's City, Heathrow, Gatwick, Luton and Stansted airports. Airlines include flyBE (tel: 0871 700 0535), bmi (tel: 0870 607 0555), Manx Airlines (tel: 0870 242 2226), Air Berlin (tel: 0870 738 8880). Aer Arann (tel: 0800 587 2324) flies to Cork twice daily on weekdays.

To get to Belfast city centre from the International Airport there is a half-hourly Airbus (leaving at 30- or 60-minute intervals on Sundays). George Best Airport has rail links to Great Victoria Street Station and a direct bus link to the city centre every 40 minutes. Taxis are plentiful from both airports.

BY SEA

Stena Line (tel: 08705 707 070) has up to 14 sailings a day between Stranraer, in Scotland, and Belfast.

Norse Merchant Ferries (tel: 0870 600 4321) operates Belfast–Liverpool and Liverpool–Dublin sailings. P&O Irish Sea (tel: 0870 2424 777) sails between Cairnryan (in Scotland) and Larne.

Getting Around

BUSES AND TRAINS

Translink (tel: 9066 6630 or visit www.translink.co.uk) operates the train and bus network in Northern Ireland. The Metro bus serves Belfast and the suburbs. Services usually start and end around the City Hall. Fares can be paid on boarding or you can buy Smartlink multi-journey tickets (travel cards are available in shops displaying the Metro sign, or from the Metro Kiosk in Donegall Square West). Goldliner Express and other Ulsterbus services to all over Northern Ireland and beyond operate from either the Europa or Laganside Bus Centres.

Northern Ireland Railways operates east to Bangor, northeast to Larne, northwest to Derry, and south to Dublin. Commuter trains from Central or Great Victoria Street Stations to Botanic provide easy access to the campus area.

TAXIS

There are taxi ranks at City Hall, the Crown Bar, airports and main stations. Drivers at Castle Junction pack London-style hackneys until full for a particular direction. An alternative is to phone a 'radio cab' such as Value Cabs (tel: 9080 9080)) from Grosvenor Road or fonaCAB (tel: 9033 3333) from the Queen's Quarter area.

BY CAR

The city has many parking lots, and on-street pay-and-display parking is generous. Donegall Place and its tributaries are pedestrianised, but only in theory. Driving is to the left; speed limits are – with clearly signed exceptions – 30mph (50km/h) in built-up areas, 60mph (95km/h) outside built-up areas and 70mph (112km/h) on motorways.

Facts for the Visitor

TIME

Belfast follows Greenwich Mean Time. During the summer, clocks are turned one hour forward.

SHOPPING HOURS

City-centre shops are generally open Mon–Sat 9.30am–5.30pm (Thurs until 9pm). Some larger stores open Sun 1–5pm. Neighbourhood stores and garage forecourt convenience shops often open much longer – 24 hours in many cases.

BANKS AND CURRENCY

Banking hours are 9.30am–4.30pm, with some village branches 10.30am–3.30pm with lunchtime closing. A few larger branches open Saturday morning. ATMs are plentiful in city centre and campus areas. Currency is the British pound sterling, but the province's banks (Bank of Ireland, First Trust, Northern and Ulster Banks) issue their own notes. Though these are also legal tender in Great Britain it is wise to change your money to Bank of England notes before leaving for the mainland. The currency of the Republic of Ireland, the euro, must be exchanged at the going rate but many big stores accept them without charging commission.

TELEPHONE NUMBERS

A single code, 028 (44 28 from outside the UK), accesses the whole of Northern Ireland and is used throughout this book.

MAIL

The main post office is in Castle Place. The Tomb Street depot, off Albert Square, provides late posting.

EMERGENCIES

Ambulance, fire, police: dial **999**.

PUBLIC HOLIDAYS

New Year's Day (1 January), St. Patrick's Day (17 March), Easter Monday, May Day (1st Monday in May), Spring Bank Holiday (last Monday in May), Orangeman's Day (12 July if not a Sunday), Summer Bank Holiday (last Monday in August), Christmas Day (25 December), Boxing Day (26 December).

TOURIST INFORMATION

The Belfast and Northern Ireland Welcome Centre (47 Donegall Place, tel: 9024 6609 or visit www.gotobelfast.com) is a one-stop tourist centre with information on accommodation, visitor attractions, tours, events and transport within Belfast and Northern Ireland as a whole. Multilingual staff can book accommodation, concerts and tours. They have a shop, left luggage facility, bureau de change and internet facilities as well as drinks machines. They also have information centres, run in conjunction with the Northern Ireland Tourist Board, at the city's two airports.

INTERNET CAFÉS

Internet Café at the Belfast Welcome Centre (47 Donegall Place, tel: 9024 6609.
Revelations (27 Shaftesbury Square, tel: 9032 0337.
Surf City Café, 207 Woodstock Road, tel: 9046 1717.

USEFUL WEBSITES

www.discovernorthernireland.com is the main site of the Northern Ireland Tourist Board. www.tourismireland.com covers the entie island, north and south. www.causewaycoastandglens.com covers the scenic east-coast drive in detail. www.familyulster.com has details of genealogy tours in Northern Ireland. www.plantsmansgardentours.com caters for those interested in garden visits. www.nitravelnews.com features travel and leisure news for Northern Ireland.

ACCOMMODATION

The Belfast Welcome Centre offers advice on availability and will book for you. For latest deals, you can also check out the Belfast and Visitor Convention Bureau website (www.gotobelfast.com). B&Bs and guesthouses are also worth seeking out, for good value, easygoing Belfast hospitality and some excellent breakfasts.

Rates can vary and there are many seasonal deals, so it may be possible to book for less than suggested here. Belfast is a popular business and conference destination in the week so weekend rates tend to be cheaper and you may be able to negotiate with some hotels.

££££ (over £150 double)

Hastings Culloden Estate and Spa, Bangor Road, tel: 9042 1066. One of Belfast's five-star hotels, it's set in 12 acres of garden overlooking the lough. A former bishop's palace, it has a £500,000 spa and fitness centre. Guests get a special deal at the nearby Royal Belfast Golf Club.

Hastings Europa Hotel, Great Victoria Street, tel: 9027 1066. Once bombed regularly, Belfast's most famous hotel has been refurbished but retains its iconic status. Good central location, opposite the famous Crown Liquor Saloon.

Hastings Stormont, Upper Newtownards Road, tel: 9065 1066. Four-star hotel overlooks Northern Ireland's seat of government, Stormont Castle. A short cab ride from Belfast City airport, it's about 4 miles (6 km) from the centre.

Hilton Belfast, 4 Lanyon Place, tel: 9027 7000. Good location by the waterfront, overlooking the Belfast Waterfront Hall and not far from the city centre. Despite its five-star status, some feel it doesn't rank among the leaders in the Hilton chain.

Hilton Templepatrick Hotel and Country Club, Castle Upton Estate, Templepatrick, tel: 9443 5500. A four-star hotel set in wooded parkland between the international airport and city centre. Popular with sporting types who can enjoy a championship golf course, swimming pool and tennis courts.

Malmaison Belfast, 34–38 Victoria Street, tel: 9022 0200. This imaginative new conversion from two beautiful Victorian seed warehouses, near the city centre and the Cathedral Quarter's artistic and gay scene, has a dramatic decor with striking bordello-themed rooms, plus popular brasserie and art deco bar.

Merchant Hotel, 35–39 Waring St, tel: 9023 4888. Formerly a richly ornamented Italianate bank headquarters, this new hotel aims is certainly the most glamorous in Belfast.

Ten Square, Ten Donegall Square South, tel: 9024 1001. A listed Victorian linen warehouse transformed into a luxury hotel with an oriental flavour. The accent on indulgence – goose down pillows, frette sheets, Bang & Olufsen plasma screens etc – attracts a following amongst Irish musos (U2, Ronan Keating, the Corrs, etc). The Grill Room and Bar is reasonable and very popular. Opposite City Hall.

Radisson SAS, The Gasworks. 3 Cromac Place. Ormeau Avenue, tel: 9043 4065. This striking modernist hotel with a fine Italian restaurant and business-friendly features has become very popular in a short space of time. Short walk to the city centre and Queen's Quarter.

£££ (over £75 double)

Ash-Rowan Town House, 12 Windsor Avenue, tel: 9066 1758. Friendly Victorian guesthouse just off Belfast's designer-label heartland, Lisburn Road and near Queen's University. Rooms and narrow hallways are crowded with owner's Sam and Evelyn Hazlett's collection of antiques and prints. Famous for superb breakfasts.

Beech Hill Country House, 23 Ballymoney Road, Craigantlet, Holywood, tel: 9042 5892. Antique furniture and fine Irish linen helped earn this grand

Holywood Hills Georgian B&B the AA Five Diamond status for quality.

Best Western Wellington Park Hotel, 21 Malone Road, tel: 9038 5050. One of Belfast's busiest hotels has good family value with children under 12 staying free. Queen's Quarter location.

Crescent Town House, 13 Lower Crescent Road, tel: 9032 3349. Stylishly restored 19th-century house in Queen's Quarter with a chic bar and popular brasserie next door.

The Old Inn, Main Street, Crawfordsburn, tel: 9185 3255. Atmospheric inn in the village of Crawfordsburn, about a 25-minute drive from the city centre. A favourite of Narnian chronicler C.S. Lewis, who grew up nearby, it's also hosted George Bush senior and, allegedly, Dick Turpin and Peter the Great. Excellent food.

Park Plaza Hotel, Belfast International Airport, tel: 9445 7000. If you've got an early flight, you can't get nearer Belfast International Airport than this well-equipped four-star hotel, a stone's throw from the departure hall.

Rayanne Country House, 60 Demesne Road, Holywood, tel: 9042 5859. Large Victorian house in Holywood with award-winning breakfasts and gourmet dinners available on request.

££ (over £50 double)

An Old Rectory, 148 Malone Road, tel: 9066 7882. Delightful upmarket Victorian guesthouse, renowned for fine breakfasts.

Days, 30 Hope Road, tel: 9024 2494. One of Belfast's biggest hotels, just down the road from the Europa, it's a good bet for family deals with rates per room.

Dukes Hotel, 65-67 University Street, tel: 9023 6666. A good-value hotel near to Queen's University and just a few minutes walk from the city centre.

Express by Holiday Inn, 106 University Road, tel: 9031 1909. Bright budget hotel close to Queen's University, it's popular with families (children stay for free) and has its own car park.

Jury's Belfast Inn, Fisherwick Place, Great Victoria St, tel: 9053 3500. Branch of the reliable budget hotel with a central location around the corner from City Hall.

Tara Lodge, 36 Cromwell Road, tel: 9059 0900. This large modern purpose-built B&B in Queen's Quarter has won awards for service.

Farset International, 466 Springfield Road, tel: 9089 9833. Upmarket hostel accommodation in west Belfast, next to a landscaped wildfowl reserve. 38 ensuite twin bedrooms, restaurant and fully-equipped self-catering kitchen.

£ (£50 and under per double)

Ark, 44 University Street, tel: 9032 9626. Four to six-bed dormitories from £10 a person at this Queen's Quarter hostel.

Arnie's Backpackers, 63 Fitzwilliam Street, tel: 9024 2867. A 22-bed Queen's Quarter hostel based in an old Victorian townhouse. From £7 a night (sharing an eight-bed dormitory) per person.

Belfast Palace Hostel, 68 Lisburn Road, tel: 9033 3367. Recently renovated Georgian house includes a huge well-equipped hostel kitchen, a dining area in a glass conservatory and drawing room. Prices range from £8.50 for a 12-bed dorm to £17 for a single room. They organise tours of Belfast and further afield.

Bowden's, 17 Sandford Avenue, tel: 9065 2213. Friendly B&B, in a cul-de-sac just off Cyprus Avenue, is a perfect base for a tour of Van Morrison's East Belfast (owner Carole Bowden is a fan).

Belfast International Youth Hostel, 22 Donegall Road, tel: 9031 5435. Just off Shaftsbury Square, this refurbished hostel offers twin, four and six bed-rooms and is open 24 hours. Continental breakfast, self-catering kitchen, laundry and TV lounge.

Queen's University. For cheap accommodation during the summer months, it's worth checking out a student room at Queen's purpose-built student village, the Elms. Call the accommodation office (9097 4525) for details. Single rooms only.

INDEX